Military Ethics for the Ex

Military Ethics for the Expeditionary Era

Edited by
Patrick Mileham and Lee Willett

THE ROYAL INSTITUTE OF
INTERNATIONAL AFFAIRS

© Royal Institute of International Affairs, 2001

First published in Great Britain in 2001 by
Royal Institute of International Affairs, 10 St James's Square,
London SW1Y 4LE
(Charity Registration No. 208 223)

Distributed worldwide by
The Brookings Institution, 1775 Massachusetts Avenue NW,
Washington DC 20036-2188, USA

British Library Cataloguing in Publication Data
A CIP catalogue record for this book is available from the British Library.

ISBN 1 86203 123 1 (hardback)
ISBN 1 86203 122 3 (paperback)

Typeset in Times by Koinonia
Printed and bound in Great Britain by the Chameleon Press
Cover design by Matthew Link
Cover photography courtesy of the UK Ministry of Defence

Contents

Contents

Contributors

Sir Paddy Ashdown KBE PC MP served in the Royal Marine Commando (Special Boat Service) in the 1960s. He worked in the Foreign and Commonwealth Office between 1970 and 1974. He was elected Member of Parliament in 1983, and led the Liberal Democrat Party between 1988 and 1999. He has paid numerous visits to the Balkans and other regions of conflict.

Dr Paul Cornish is Newton Sheehy lecturer, Centre of International Studies, University of Cambridge, and served in the Royal Tank Regiment.

Major-General Arthur Denaro CBE took up the position of General Officer Commanding 5th Division in January 2001, and was previously Commandant of the Royal Military Academy, Sandhurst. He commanded the Queen's Royal Irish Hussars Armoured Regiment during the Gulf War.

Brigadier General Loup Francart commands the 2nd Armoured Chasseurs Regiment and was Deputy Chief of Operations, 12th Light Armoured Division, in the French Army. He is currently Research Director at the Institut de Relations Internationales et Stratégiques, Paris.

Colonel Anthony Hartle US Army is Head of the Department of English, US Military Academy, West Point. He commanded a battalion of the 101st Airborne Division before retiring from the US Army. He is the author of *Moral Issues in Military Decision Making* (1990).

William Hopkinson worked in both the Treasury and the Ministry of Defence, where he was Head of Defence Arms Control Unit and Assistant Under-Secretary of State for Policy with responsibilities for NATO, the Western European Union, and bilateral relations with other nations. He joined the Royal Institute of International Affairs in 1997 and was Deputy Director until 2000.

Dr Michael Ignatieff is a writer and television documentary presenter and has held numerous academic posts in Canada, Britain, France and the United States. His publications include *The Warrior's Honor: Ethnic War and the Modern Conscience* (1998) and *Virtual War: Kosovo and Beyond* (2000).

Colonel Paul Maillet is a Canadian Air Force officer and Director of Defence Ethics for the Department of National Defence and the Canadian Forces, organizations of over 100,000 military, civilian, reserve and cadet personnel. Over the past four years, he has been responsible for the development and implementation of a military value-based ethics programme.

General James P. McCarthy USAF is the Olin Professor of National Security at the USAF Academy, Colorado Springs. He served for 35 years in the Unites States Air Force, commanding a fighter squadron in Vietnam and two bomber wings before becoming Deputy Commander in Chief, US European Command. He has served on numerous high-level committees in the Pentagon, US Senate and business, professional and non-profit organizations.

Patrick Mileham is Governor at the University of Paisley and Associate Fellow at the Royal Institute of International Affairs. He served in the Royal Tank Regiment. His recent publications include *Transforming Corporate Leadership* (with Keith Spacie) and *Ethical Dilemmas of Military Interventions* (edited with Lee Willett).

Marisa Rodríguez Mojón is Professor of Political Science, Suffolk University, Boston MA, and teaches at the School of Higher National Defence Studies, Spanish Ministry of Defence.

Professor Adam Roberts is a Fellow of Balliol College Oxford, where he is Montague Burton Professor of International Relations. He taught at the London School of Economics from 1968 to 1981. His *Documents on the Laws of War* (with Richard Guelff) is the standard work on the subject, and he is also the co-editor of *United Nations, Divided World: The UN's Roles in International Relations* (1993).

General Sir Rupert Smith KCB DSO OBE QGM served in the Parachute Regiment. He commanded 1st British Division in the Gulf War and UNPROFOR in Bosnia-Herzegovina in 1995. He is currently Deputy Supreme Allied Commander Europe, NATO forces.

Dr Lee Willett works on the Military Science Programme at the Royal United Services Institute for Defence Studies. At the time this book was written, he was Leverhulme Research Fellow at the Centre for Security studies at the University of Hull and was seconded as a Research Associate to the Naval Staff Directorate in the Ministry of Defence. Dr Willett has published widely on the future of the Royal Navy and its submarine service, as well as on military ethics.

Foreword

I am delighted to be able to contribute the foreword to this collection of papers from the international conference on military ethics, hosted by the Royal Institute of International Affairs. It is a timely volume, addressing significant new challenges for military forces in the post-Cold War world. In every circumstance, we look to our armed forces to carry out their duties to the highest professional standard. British servicemen and servicewomen continue to meet ably these necessarily high expectations – most recently in Kosovo, East Timor and Sierra Leone.

For these latest operations, they have taken on the new roles and tasks discussed in these papers. In the process, they have acted selflessly, honestly and impartially. They have, of course, confronted very real physical danger. And in these new roles, they have also faced the new moral and ethical challenges debated at this conference. Their practical example in successfully facing these new challenges is complemented by the academic debate which this volume takes forward.

The conference itself drew together an impressive list of participants, from over 20 countries. I am pleased that this volume, incorporating a broad range of views, will now take these issues to an even wider audience.

Robin Cook
Secretary of State for Foreign and Commonwealth Affairs

Preface

The subject of military ethics is now at the heart of international security policy and the practical application of military power to conflicts and disasters around the world. The use of military force in its traditional war-fighting mode is an instrument whose bluntness is increasingly open to challenge. Meanwhile, military intervention in peacekeeping, peace enforcement, stabilization and humanitarian operations is fraught with many dangers. Proposed military 'solutions' by well-meaning outside powers can easily become part of, and exacerbate, the problem. The Royal Institute of International Affairs accepted the intellectual challenge of launching work on this subject because military authority and methods of conducting intervention operations in the new expeditionary era have become matters of deep debate and literally vital importance.

This book derives from the international conference entitled 'Ethics in the Expeditionary Era: The Ethical Challenges for the New Roles and Tasks of the Armed Forces', held at the Royal Military Academy Sandhurst, United Kingdom, on 11–12 November 1999. The conference was the second in a series of events, following a seminar held at the RIIA in November 1998.[1]

I am grateful to all the speakers and participants in the conference, and to those who worked behind the scenes to ensure its success. I am also particularly grateful to Patrick Mileham and Lee Willett, whose unstinting efforts saw to the detail of the conference and pulled this book together. I hope this publication will take forward the project in Britain and internationally.

William Hopkinson
Former Deputy Director
Royal Institute of International Affairs

---

[1] The papers presented at the seminar were published in P. Mileham and L. Willett (eds), *Ethical Dilemmas of Military Interventions* (London: Royal Institute of International Affairs, 1999).

Acknowledgments

This project's genesis goes back to 1995, when the 'ethos of the British army' was being formally addressed and debated for an Army Board paper.

Many people have contributed to the development of the project from which this book has derived. William Hopkinson, Former Deputy Director and Director of Studies of the RIIA, provided the project's initial stimulus and has headed the entire process. The editors' tasks have been made considerably easier by the contribution of the steering committee: Lord Roper, Major General Antony Palmer; Brigadier Sebastian Roberts OBE; Colonel Archie Miller-Bakewell; Group Captain Stuart Peach RAF; Group Captain Peter Gray RAF; Group Captain John Thomas RAF; Captain Peter Hore RN; and Wing Commander Phillip Greville RAF. Major General Arthur Denaro CBE, Commandant, graciously offered the Royal Military Academy, Sandhurst as a splendid venue for such a prestigious gathering. His staff, Captain Rupert Greenwood and Captain Damian Briggs-Wilson QRIH, also provided generous support and assistance. Major Jeremy Bennett pulled together the practicalities of the conference itself, patiently negotiating the administrative minefields that lay in our path. Commander Chuck 'Silver' Lewis United States Navy (Retired), Lieutenant Commander Victoria Turner United States Navy (US Naval War College) and Colonel Charles Myers (US Air Force Academy) provided much assistance in planning the conference concept. Our speakers and delegates prompted and took part in an intense and lively debate, which we hope is accurately and fully reported and reflected in these pages. The staff at Sandhurst, from catering staff to transport drivers, proved to be crucial in the smooth running of the event. The conference and this book would not have been possible without considerable financial support from several very important sources. The editors wish to thank here the External Relations Office at the North Atlantic Treaty Organization; the Foreign and Commonwealth Office; Rolls Royce plc; the Head of Defence Studies, Royal Navy; and the British embassy, Madrid.

Finally, the editors wish to convey particular thanks to three people, without whom the project would not have reached its conclusion. Laura Hamilton, administrator to the International Security Programme at the RIIA, has provided the editors with more assistance than politely could have been requested. Margaret May and Kim Mitchell at Chatham House had the patience and singleminded attention that has brought this book to publication. The editors' debt to them is unquantifiable.

The issue of military ethics remains crucial in contemporary debates about the use of force and what it can achieve. The editors hope that this book can make a contribution to a greater understanding of the challenges this issue poses.

Patrick Mileham
Lee Willett

1 Introduction: the ethical minefield

Arthur Denaro

Let me explain very quickly why the Royal Military Academy, Sandhurst is so special to me as commandant, and to those who work and serve here. First, it is a beautiful place. Our buildings are steeped in history, particularly in the Royal Memorial Chapel, where the names of all those cadets commissioned from Sandhurst who have died in the service of their country are recorded, on the pillars for the First World War and in a book of remembrance, a page of which is turned each Sunday, for the Second World War. Another book, which is still open, is for those who have died since then.

The second reason why Sandhurst is so special is the quality of its civilian staff, and in particular its academic staff. It teaches the cadets the role of armed force in world politics and the place of the army in society today. Nothing could be more important or more appropriate as we approach the subject that we are about to discuss.

The third reason is that its military staff is chosen from among the best of its peers throughout the army. The Chief of General Staff directs me to 'train tomorrow's officers with the best officers and senior ranks of today'. That is what the members of Sandhurst's staff are.

The fourth, and most important, reason, is the cadets themselves. They come from all over the British Isles. They come with different baggage from different backgrounds, different experiences, different upbringings and different educations. The only thing that all these 700 cadets have in common with each other is the fact that they have been selected to come here on their potential to lead and command soldiers in these very difficult and dangerous days. They are here for only a year, and we focus for that year on leadership and command. Unlike St Cyr, West Point and the Herres Schule in Germany, whose cadets spend four or even five years studying for a degree, 85 per cent of our cadets are graduates; the other 15 per cent

1

come either from the ranks of the army or from what I would call the 'university of life'. That is why this place, the cradle of our officer corps, is different and special and why we are delighted to host this conference.

The subject of military ethics is very complex, very difficult and yet absolutely vital for us soldiers to grasp. There is nothing new about the ethical debate or about expeditionary warfare; it is an age-old agenda. In the nineteenth century gentleman cadets were leaving this academy to take part in expeditions to rescue hostages from mad emperors in Ethiopia or to save besieged residencies in India. Across the Channel they were leaving St Cyr to join expeditions to rescue Christian communities from Muslim fanatics in Beirut or to punish the Annamese in Indochina for their abuse of European missionaries. Nor were these actions always unilateral. The British, the French and other European powers supported expeditions to suppress piracy in the Mediterranean, the Caribbean and the East Indies and the slave trade in the Atlantic and the Indian Ocean. Multinational expeditions were the rule rather than the exception in the nineteenth century. That which marched on Peking in 1900 – British, Americans, French, Russians, Germans, Austrians, Italians and Japanese – was by no means untypical.

Most of the soldiers who took part in these expeditions did not question their purpose. They believed themselves to be the spearhead of a superior civilization, both technologically and, more importantly, ethically. Most believed it was their moral duty to intervene to suppress what they had been taught to see as barbarism, to stop the Ashanti or the Zulu or the Tuareg terrorizing their neighbours. In so doing they believed they were bringing the benefits of Christian civilization to the benighted heathen. There were exceptions, of course. Colonel Durnford, who was to be killed at Isandwalana, believed the expedition to Zululand to be motivated by imperial expansionism rather than real concern about the depredations of the Zulu. A young officer from my own regiment, the Fourth Hussars, in the Sudan in October 1898, Lieutenant Winston Churchill, regarded the treatment of the Dervish wounded after the battle of Omdurman as an affront to civilization. But such misgivings were not common.

In Britain, domestic support for such expeditions was more variable. Manchester liberals such as Richard Cobden and John Bright, and later the great Liberal prime minister Gladstone and the Marxist economist Hobson, usually opposed expeditionary interventions. But at the time they did not represent the opinion of the majority. The cost of expeditionary warfare in those days was relatively low both economically and in terms of casualties, and the leaders of popular opinion – the bishops, the historians, the biologists, the journalists – reinforced and expanded the notion that such operations were the moral duty of great civilized powers.

Nowadays we inhabit a very different moral universe. For most of the twentieth century, our countries were engaged in the fighting of or the preparation for total war. To our dismay and disbelief, we discovered in the course of that century that even those who subscribe to Judaeo-Christian ethics are capable of a barbarism against which the depredations of the Ashanti or the Zulu pale into insignificance. Thus the debate on military ethics did not stop in the twentieth century. Instead, the revelation that armies composed of educated citizen soldiers from advanced industrial civilizations could behave with a barbarism worthy of Genghis Khan or Tamerlane intensified the debate and led ultimately to a strengthening of the precepts governing behaviour during and after combat. The result is that more is expected of the soldier and, in particular, the young officer in terms of ethical behaviour than ever before. Unlike our great-grandfathers, the great majority of us no longer believe that our civilization is superior to that of others.

Or do we? Like our great-grandfathers we live in a world in which pressures to intervene, to put things to rights, to rescue oppressed minorities, to save starving children and to prevent massacres are frequently intense. Thus we have a huge problem. Although we no longer have the moral certainty and the cultural arrogance which legitimized expeditions in the nineteenth century, occasionally we must nevertheless undertake such expeditions.

One question this conference will wish to address is, how do we justify such expeditions? Realists would say that no intervention can ever be justified unless one's vital national interests are at stake. If national interests are at stake, intervention might not necessarily support the party which appears to be the most injured or to have the most justice on its side. Public opinion, so well informed by the media, might be enraged. Public opinion can exert huge pressure, particularly on politically weak governments. But such storms are usually of short duration. Should governments try to ride out these storms? Or can we arrive at universally understood moral criteria which could and would invariably justify

3

intervention? Idealists would say that we can and we must. The former leader of the Liberal Democrats, the Rt Hon. Sir Paddy Ashdown MP, no doubt will guide us through this debate.

I said at the beginning of this introduction that the debate over ethics and the employment of military force has been going on since the beginning of recorded history. So has the search for criteria to support the *casus belli*. The conduct of Europe's first multinational expeditionary operations, otherwise known as the Crusades, provided an enormous stimulus to that debate. St Augustine had argued that God's law of love obliged Christians to come to the aid of others, thereby justifying the use of force. Thomas Aquinas developed St Augustine's work and gave us the list, subsequently expanded in the sixteenth and the early seventeenth centuries, of the criteria for the use of force that we all know so well: legitimate authority; a just cause; the right intention; proportionality; a last resort; and a reasonable hope of success. Did we not hear all these churned out frequently in recent months over Kosovo?

It is easy to show that leaders down the centuries have deviated from these criteria. What is more remarkable is that most, even Adolf Hitler, attempted to legitimize their actions by reference to them. But can the criteria for a just war have any relevance in informing military ethics in this latest period of expeditionary operations? This issue will be pursued by the distinguished scholar of international law from Oxford University, Professor Adam Roberts. The ethical considerations involved in deciding whether or not to launch an intervention are complex. Equally difficult are those which govern the behaviour of soldiers once they are on the ground.

As I have noted above, one of the paradoxical results of the barbarities of the twentieth century has been a strengthening of the laws of war. But what if the expedition has not gone to a war? Most modern expeditions are classified in that grey area known variously as peace-support, implementation or stabilization operations. The soldier is expected to observe not only the rules of war but also the rules of engagement, which will vary from expedition to expedition. Some of them will seem to make little sense to him or to critical observers. As examples, I put forward three experiences from my own time as a soldier.

The first was in Dhofar in the early 1970s. After two days' lying in ambush one of my team of Omani irregulars stood up to pray just as we saw the enemy approaching, Not surprisingly, the enemy moved away and out of range. Hugely irritated, I questioned the soldier, only to find that his brother was one of the enemy. Two days later the whole enemy patrol surrendered and came over to the sultan's side – we discovered it was twice as effective to recruit the enemy as it was to kill him!

Later on, in the Gulf war, suddenly the Iraqis, particularly those in the trenches, were surrendering. Yet behind them they were deploying some of the tanks of their armoured divisions. Should my soldiers continue to fight, to drive on, to hit with hard aggressive action as they had been trained to do, or should they show restraint? This was a very difficult moral dilemma for the young tank commander.

In a third experience, one which many of us here have seen and been through both in Bosnia and in Kosovo, we have stood outraged in the midst of the most inhuman behaviour without the absolute authority to intervene and stop 'ethnic cleansing'. Yet again the decision was for the young commander, the platoon commander, the troop leader on the ground. It is immensely difficult and quite wrong that they should be put in this position; thus it is incredibly important that we address the issues of moral duty, direction and orders for these complex situations.

The behaviour of all soldiers is governed by laws, conventions and customs and by their particular training – and now, of course, by the presence of the media. All this can make life extremely difficult for the soldier on the ground, but it also makes life nearly impossible for the higher commander. After his service in Bosnia in 1993 General Lewis Mackenzie, who was addressing our instructors at the Army Staff College, pointed to a picture of General Philippe Morillon which had been projected onto the screen. Mackenzie warned his audience that service in Bosnia had destroyed Morillon's career and his own career, and that, because it was the way of the future, unless the audience were very careful it might well destroy their careers too!

The problem, as one commentator noted, was that although the men who become generals are by no means necessarily repositories of human virtue, they are certainly not cowards. Yet the new roles which the expeditionary era has imposed on senior commanders, have frequently produced a conflict between deep-seated codes of military honour – the ethical aspect of command – and the need to behave with circumspection – to temporize, to look the other way. These latter are not the lessons taught at West Point, at St Cyr or at Sandhurst.

Can our discussions here chart a course through this ethical minefield? I am sure we all hope so. The challenges of command in this environment can make the senior officer wish he were in a more straightforward war. I noted earlier the new pressures these operations place on soldiers. It is the responsibility of their officers, and ultimately of the senior commander, to command effectively throughout them. Thus this conference must debate and conclude that the absolute requirement is for all practitioners and theorists, and all governors and teachers, constantly to review their position on the ethics of war. Ethics is at the core of young officers' education, because they are the ones who have to command and lead their fine soldiers in these difficult and dangerous times.

2 What political circumstances justify military intervention?

Paddy Ashdown

I have been asked to contribute my views on 'ethics in the expeditionary era' and on 'what political circumstances justify military intervention?'. In considering the Commandant's very interesting introduction, I realized that I would probably want to go just a little further and address what I think is the developing new doctrine for intervention in an ethical context. I also want to set this discussion within what I believe is a necessary broader framework talking about the creation and function of global institutions, of which the capacity to intervene internationally is only one part.

Answers to theoretical questions are always best found in practical examples. The latest examples of practical experience of intervention to which we, in this part of the world, have access are Kosovo and Bosnia. Incidentally, I do not think that, successful though it was, NATO fought a flawless campaign in Kosovo – very far from it. There are serious lessons for NATO to learn, and some of them are addressed by General Sir Rupert Smith in Chapter 6. Lord Robertson, the NATO Secretary-General, has a very big job to do if we are to learn some of the lessons of the Kosovo conflict.

At the risk of being slightly political, I do not believe, either, that our own government's conduct of the Kosovo campaign was absolutely flawless. We were a little late in arriving at the realization that ground troops would be needed, and I found some of the Ministry of Defence briefings a little too didactic. But I have no doubt, having been mildly critical, that overall the role played by the British government was crucial to the eventual success of the whole Kosovo operation. The prime minister played a key role in stiffening the backbone of our allies, maybe even influencing the US administration. Had this not been so – had it not been for the rather remarkable and special determination of our government and our armed forces to see the operation through – then I think the outcome of the Kosovo operation could have been very different, with immensely damaging consequences for NATO, for the structure of international law and, of course, for the people of Kosovo itself. I apologize for taking a somewhat nationalistic approach in front of an international audience. Yet it is well worth while recording that, in my view, Kosovo was a successful NATO operation, and I think we also followed the right policies.

In addressing the subject of what military circumstances justify intervention, I shall begin with a brief story. Almost exactly a year ago, and several months before the war started, I was on one of my visits to Kosovo. I was actually in the Suva Reka region just south of Pristina, in the little villages that dot the hillsides of this pleasant, primitive farming area. I was there as, in an act of mediaeval barbarity, the villagers were being bombarded, looted and burnt by the tanks, artillery and soldiers, if that is what you can call them, of the Serb army. Suddenly, amid the mayhem and the noise and the misery of plain people, I noticed two very curious little things: every single Albanian village, however small, had its own graveyard and every Albanian house, however poor, had its own satellite dish. But while the graves pointed according to Muslim tradition at Mecca, the satellite dishes pointed at Murdoch. Well, I use that for alliteration. Probably it was not Murdoch, but the BBC, but you get the point. I started thinking which of these two facts would influence these people most in the future – the way in which their tradition requires them to bury their dead or the way in which they get their news, their information and their entertainment. What I was seeing even here in the hills of Kosovo was an example of what I believe is the most important fact of our age, the globalization of power. The old political 'settlement' is breaking down. Under that old compact, the compact between the citizen and the state, national governments offered security and prosperity in return for supreme power at home and the unchallenged right to speak for their citizens abroad. That settlement is being irresistibly reshaped by the force of events and, in particular, by the process of the globalization of power.

In some senses, of course, this is not new. We have long understood that our security could no longer be assured by national governments alone. That is why we pooled our sovereignty in NATO and why we were right to do so. But nowadays this trend extends to much more than security. Our prosperity too can depend on what happens beyond our borders and beyond the reach and influence of our own governments. Nowadays a market crash in Taiwan means a factory closure in Tyneside. The managing director of a car-making enterprise in South Korea can have a greater impact on unemployment in south Wales than the secretary of state for Wales. A trade war about bananas means job losses in the Scottish Borders. In the free and increasingly global market a national government alone can no more guarantee jobs for all, whatever our chancellor might say, than it can guarantee sunshine on Sundays. Nor can a government guarantee a clean environment. A nuclear accident in Ukraine means contamination in Snowdonia and so on. No longer does any country have absolute sovereignty, as you might have argued in the days of the nation-state in the eighteenth and nineteenth centuries. This is extremely important because it means that we are no longer totally independent; we are increasingly interdependent. There is a set of rules to be devised and followed.

In history, whenever power migrates outside the structures established to control it – and that is what we are seeing now – change happens, and very often disruptive change. So it was with the barons of Magna Carta; so it was with Cromwell's Parliament and the King; so it was with the growth of industrial power and the great Reform Act; and so now, as power migrates and accumulates, often at frightening speed, in the hands of the global players. These global players include the commodity traders, the Internet operators, the satellite broadcasters, the multinational traders. They are all unfettered and unconstrained by the structures of any government or by any ideology, or any belief, or any particular culture – those things from which, incidentally, we often draw our national identity in the first place. Here is what seems to me an inescapable fact, that power is moving at an increasingly fast pace beyond the confines of the nation-state and is rapidly making many of its institutions irrelevant. Incidentally, though it may be uncomfortable to face up to, one of those threatened institutions may well be our national process of democracy itself – as we see from growing apathy in the ballot box. What is the point of voting for your government if it too is powerless in the face of those other global powers for which you cannot vote?

That is the question, and here is the conclusion. We are going to have to start thinking about global government, and about starting to invest more power in global institutions. The nation-states, their governments and above all their politicians are frankly going to hate it but the longer they leave it, the more powerless they will become, the more chaos and destruction will be caused and the more painful will be the transition. We are going to need new doctrines and practices for international intervention in places like Kosovo and East Timor, new structures to enforce the control of global pollution and new means to harness the power of the global market while limiting its capacity to destabilize and disrupt.

I do not have time here to cover all these matters and you did not ask me to anyway. Thus for a moment I am going deliberately to concentrate on one of them, and it touches very much on the subject which we are discussing here – the new rules we shall need for intervention.

First, let me address for a moment a national agenda. I think Britain and this government now have a unique opportunity to take a leading role in the process of creating, or helping to create, the new structures for government which we shall need for global stability in the future. Our prime minister and foreign secretary enjoy, quite properly after the Kosovo operation, a high level of respect in the international community. We in Britain are leaders and key participants in what might be described as the three key circles of global influence: the Security Council, the European Union and the Commonwealth. This gives us an international network of unparalleled breadth in which to work. We still have a world-view which our fellow European countries, with the exception of France, probably still lack. Our military are world leaders in the practice of post-imperial peacekeeping and our foreign service is experienced, influential and well respected. These combine to make what I think is a truly unique set of assets with which Britain could give a lead in strengthening systems of global governments. Then, at last, we might have an answer to Dean Acheson's old but accurate jibe that Britain was a nation that had lost an empire but had yet to find a role.

I shall now turn from the theoretical to the practical and try to find an answer to one of the key components of what I regard as this necessary new structure of global governments. Again, let us go back to Kosovo. In April I visited the small Albanian town of Kukes, just a few kilometres from the Kosovan border. I wandered among the refugees, listening to their stories and trying to absorb the scale of the humanitarian disaster that they had endured. Among the things I heard, one comment struck me particularly. It came from a 20-year-old Kosovar Albanian girl. She said,

'I was always told that the West only went to war for land or oil, yet here is NATO fighting for me'. Of course, she was right. In most international conflicts refugees are the by-product of war, its forgotten leftovers. Kosovo was arguably the first war in which the refugees became the purpose of the war and indeed the determinant of victory or defeat. It was defeat if we did not get them back to their land and homes. Yet this simple fact – that NATO was fighting not for territorial rights but for human rights – has far-reaching consequences for the international community, its institutions and, I would argue, its laws. Above all, it has huge implications for the United Nations and its charter, which is based on the inviolability of sovereign states and, through that, for the practice (if not the principle) of non-intervention in their internal affairs.

Simply put, the stand which the international community found itself taking against the human rights atrocities committed in Kosovo turns this doctrine completely on its head. Will it be respect for human rights or respect for national sovereignty? I suspect that there will increasingly be times when the international community is going to have to choose between the two. If you believe, as I do, that the campaign to reverse Milosevic's policy of ethnic cleansing was just and right – even if there were some flaws in its execution – then logically you have to question whether the assertion of domestic sovereignty in Article 2, paragraph 7 of the UN Charter can be seen to hold any more.

What is needed is a new approach which, although still based on the presumption of non-intervention, sets out clearly those circumstances in which that intervention can be challenged or altered. In essence we need to define the circumstances in which the international community has a right, if not a moral obligation, to defend people from oppression when the oppressor is their own, sometimes even their own elected, government.

How do we identify such circumstances? I would like to suggest four criteria for international intervention. I readily admit that the first three are matters of principle and that the fourth is a matter of sheer practicality.

1. Have all available diplomatic avenues for resolution of domestic violations of human rights been exhausted?
2. Is the state in question acting in gross violation of international law or the Universal Declaration of Human Rights?
3. Does this action threaten wider stability in the region, for instance

by creating floods of refugees or seriously degrading the environment of the area?

4. Is intervention militarily and politically practicable?

If the answer to any of these four questions is 'no', then intervention is not justified. But if the answer to all four of them is 'yes', then I would argue that it is appropriate for intervention to proceed, in accordance with international law.

These criteria through practical international principles universally applied (with however much difficulty) would do much, I think, to promote transparency, objectivity and consistency in future decisions on military intervention. Perhaps just as importantly, their application would do much both to reassure those who suspect Western intervention to be based on hegemonic or imperialistic ambitions and to ensure that such campaigns are based on the firm foundation of international law and practice. Of course, these objective tests may still have to pass through the subjective filter of Security Council analysis. That will always be preferable, but it may not be necessary in every circumstance, as I shall seek to explain in a moment.

Having defined the circumstances in which intervention in the internal jurisdiction of a sovereign state by or on behalf of the international community is justified, we must resolve next how and by whom it might be mounted: in short, who is to police the increasingly interdependent world in which we live? The answer to this, as we saw in the Balkans recently, is that the UN will, in my view, continue to act as the guardian of international law but will increasingly subcontract the peacemaking role to others. It seems to me there are three candidates for the peacemaking task: one is the UN itself; the second is regional security groupings; and the third is what might be termed 'coalitions of the willing'. Until we manage to reform the UN – I hope we shall one day, although I cannot see the political will to do so now – and give it a genuine peacekeeping and peacemaking ability, I feel that its forces will be used only in the last resort as 'peacemakers'. Any of you who saw the early stages of the Bosnian operation will know why. I rather doubt whether, in the light of that experience and others elsewhere, states are going to commit their young men and women to armed conflict in the most difficult circumstances of all under the command of a UN force which, to put it at its best, is supported by a rather ineffective command structure. The UN simply does not have a command structure, a logistic network, intelligence provision or even a certainty of troops of adequate calibre to conduct the most difficult of military tasks. Bosnia exemplified this all too clearly. I wish it were not so, and if we were able seriously to reform and strengthen the UN's peacekeeping structures, then one day perhaps it will not be so. Some countries, Britain among them, are already taking corrective action, pledging readily available troops for the UN. But for now we must acknowledge that the UN is under-equipped.

That means that the main burden in the near future of acting to uphold the UN's law will, in my view, fall upon regional security organizations – NATO in Kosovo, the Economic Community of West African States (ECOWAS) in Sierra Leone, and South-East Asian security forces in a rather less formalized way in East Timor. If so, then one of the UN's tasks ought to be to encourage the growth, cohesion and capability of such regional structures. Another ought to be to ensure that when such alliances act, they do so preferably with the backing of a Security Council resolution. But if this is unachievable (as in Kosovo), regional alliances must act scrupulously within the body of international law and particularly its most important text, the UN Charter itself. When regional structures cannot act, it must be left to 'coalitions of the willing' to do so, subject always to the same constraints of international law as regional security organizations. The alliance which was assembled during the Gulf War is an example of this, even if not a perfect one in practice.

As I have already said, Security Council resolutions are desirable to support such actions. But, given the interplay of forces and the effect of the veto in the Security Council, common sense indicates that an absolute requirement for a Security Council resolution would in some circumstances be a recipe for inaction rather than action. This might well have been the case in Kosovo and elsewhere. The point here is this: international law is enshrined in many places other than Security Council resolutions; it is also to be found in, among other places, pre-existing bilateral agreements; the Geneva Convention; the laws governing armed conflict; and, not least, the UN Charter itself.

It seems to me that in this way the UN acts as the author and guardian of international law, even if it subcontracts enforcement to others. But the UN's role is not finished once military intervention is over. It also has a role as a validator and protector of the peace it has sponsored. It is no doubt annoying to NATO that the UN has moved in to oversee the stabilization and renewal of Kosovo, but in my view this is nevertheless a good thing. It diminishes the fear of colonization, and it provides a better context for conciliation and stronger multilateral guarantees of lasting peace than would the continued domination of the region by the military machine which monopolized the conflict.

So far this has all been about what could be called the theory of international relations. My final point is about deeply practical military realities on the ground. If the kind of operation we saw in Kosovo really is fought for and about humanitarian reasons, as we claimed at the time, then humanitarian issues have to be at the heart of the military operation. In the old post-colonial wars in which I got my early experience as a soldier, we used to say that we were 'operating in support of the civil power'. In Bosnia, Kosovo and other similar recent conflicts, the forces involved have been operating in support of the international power. This means that the international power effectively has to be the tasking authority, particularly in relation to humanitarian assistance. The junior military commanders I met in Bosnia in the early days recognized this well and had swiftly adapted to their new circumstances the procedures they learnt in the internal security operations of the post-colonial era. Frequently they accepted that the United Nations High Commissioner for Refugees (UNHCR) was their effective tasking authority in the early days of the conflict, and it was remarkable to see how they developed the custom and practice to make that happen. However, the message is, I think, less well understood further up the military tree, where the implications for senior officers can be quite uncomfortable. They too will have to acknowledge that if the purpose of an intervention is international, the international community has to have a role in their decision-making too, however encumbering this might be from time to time.

I have looked forward briefly to the twenty-first century, to what I think is the dominant fact of our age – the globalization of power and the need to create global institutions to match it. In concluding I shall look back to the nineteenth century and use the words of perhaps the father of internationalism and, I think, this country's greatest prime minister so far – William Gladstone. I shall quote for you the words he used in the second Midlothian campaign when he sought, successfully, to form the country's new government at a time when Britain was gripped by a jingoistic fervour as powerful as during the Falklands War – over the invasion, our invasion, of Afghanistan. You might think of those villages in Kosovo when you hear these words but I hope you will also be aware that Gladstone's words constituted a set of moral principles for him at the end of the nineteenth century. These words are, I believe, the beginnings of a code of survival for us at the beginning of the twenty-first century. He said to this country – and he had the courage to say it and it had the courage to elect him on that basis:

> Do not forget that the sanctity of life in the hill villages of Afghanistan amongst the winter snows is no less inviolate in the eyes of Almighty God as can be your own. Do not forget that He who made you brothers in the same flesh and blood bound you by the laws of mutual love and that love is not confined to the shores of this island but it passes across the whole surface of the earth encompassing the greatest along with the meanest in its unmeasured scope.

Ethics for him, survival for us.

3 The changing form and function of the laws of war

Adam Roberts

I have an uncle whose death in the First World War is commemorated in the chapel at Sandhurst. This is a moment to commemorate a life that might have been. The ghastly carnage of the First World War, of which the names in the chapel are a frightening reminder, is also a reminder of the limits of the subject about which I am going to speak, the laws of war. There had been a good deal of progressive development in that field before the First World War, especially at the Hague Conferences of 1899 and of 1907, in which this country played a major part. These conferences produced many treaties by which states became bound, but that body of law was, sad to say, largely irrelevant to the dreadful carnage that ensued. It is not possible to say that the disasters of the First World War were all due to violations of the law. These events in many ways exposed the limits of that body of law. Speaking as an International Relations academic who has an interest in law, I have a firm belief in testing law against practice, understanding how it works in practice and the complexity of its various functions.

The 1990s saw a hugely increased interest in the whole field of the laws of armed conflict. Sometimes this field is given other names. A good deal of international diplomatic and NGO practice refers to it as international humanitarian law rather than the laws of war. Yet, whatever label it comes under, there is no doubt that the subject has acquired increased salience, partly because wars are now very visible both to the electorate of countries that are taking part in them, and to those states that are not directly involved.

The increased interest has been due to the fact that in some wars of our era, the laws of war had a positive function. This is the perception, for example, among many of the armed forces that contributed to the 1990–1 Gulf War coalition. The application of the laws of war in that conflict was not free from controversy or difficulty. Yet the law did provide useful guidelines for the conduct of military operations.

Events in several conflicts, and the reporting of them, have contributed to a growing public awareness of war crimes. This in turn has led to the creation of two international tribunals, for Yugoslavia and Rwanda, and also to the Rome Statute of the International Criminal Court. There has also been a growing awareness of the pointless destruction caused by anti-personnel mines and the need to control their use. All this is set against a post-Cold War background in which it seems that as preoccupation with the ideological confrontation between East and West has declined, preoccupation with human rights and humanitarian issues generally has increased. That, of course, feeds back into laws of war issues.

As the laws of war are sometimes perceived by some as high-minded injunctions that operate against state interests, it is worth recalling the simple fact that the 1949 Geneva Conventions have as many parties as any treaty. I do not know of any treaty that has more than the 188 parties that are currently bound by the 1949 Geneva Conventions. The UN Charter, incidentally, also has 188 parties. Furthermore, there has been a remarkable increase in the last decade in the number of parties to the sometimes controversial 1977 Geneva Protocol I, that governs international armed conflict. On 1 July 1988 it had 76 parties; now it has 155 parties, including all the NATO members except Turkey, France and the United States.

However – and this is where the aspect of my title on the changing 'form' as well as 'function' of the laws of war comes in – there were many new developments in the 1990s that have changed the character of the laws of war in significant ways. Four new treaties entered into force in the decade. The United Kingdom is a party to all of them. They are:

1. The 1994 Convention on the Safety of United Nations and Associated Personnel. One can argue as to whether this is a laws of war treaty in a strict sense or whether it is something else, but it certainly has an impact on the laws of war and on the conduct of armed forces in a large number of ways.
2. and 3. The two protocols to the 1980 Convention on Certain Conventional Weapons. One, namely, Protocol IV, deals with 'Blinding Laser Weapons', the second, (amended Protocol II), concerns 'Prohibitions or Restrictions Relating to the Use of Anti-Personnel

Mines'. The former concluded in 1995 and the latter in 1996; both have entered into force, and they have 40 and 38 parties respectively.

4. The 1997 Ottawa Convention on the Prohibition of the Use, Stockpiling, Production and Transfer of Anti-Personnel Mines and their Destruction. This has 84 parties.

There are in addition two new treaties from the 1990s which are not yet in force. The 1998 Rome Statute of the International Criminal Court contains a very full itemization of war crimes, including crimes that are deemed to be war crimes in civil wars. The 1998 Second Hague Protocol on the Protection of Cultural Property seeks to give some teeth to the 1954 convention on the same subject, reinforcing its application to civil wars.

It is not just in the old-fashioned form of treaties that there have been new developments. There have also been a number of other developments which have not been in treaty form, often for quite revealing reasons. There is the Statute of the International Criminal Tribunal for the Former Yugoslavia, approved by the UN Security Council in 1993. It was felt best to implement this statute in the form of a Security Council Resolution and not a treaty because treaty negotiations would have been hopelessly long-drawn-out, would have resulted in all kinds of objections and difficulties and would have been likely to prove inconclusive. Then there is an updated, informal summary of the law applicable to naval warfare in the form of the 1994 San Remo Manual on International Law Applicable to Armed Conflicts at Sea. There is another informal updating of the law in the form of the 1994 UN General Assembly Resolution on the Protection of the Environment in Times of Armed Conflict. This seeks to relate existing law to a particular and concrete problem. Then, also from 1994, there is the Statute of the International Criminal Tribunal for Rwanda, again adopted by the Security Council. There is too the Advisory Opinion of the International Court of Justice on Nuclear Weapons, from 1996. In August 1999 the UN Secretary-General's Bulletin on the Application of International Humanitarian Law to UN forces was promulgated.

Some of these documents, including the last, suggest that the law may be developed and applied in forms different from treaties. This is one important innovation in recent years. Within the United Nations a great deal of thought was given to how the application of the law to UN forces should be promulgated, and in the end it was done in the legally binding form of the Secretary-General's bulletin, rather than by attempting a huge and open-ended negotiation. Several of these documents, whether treaties or other types of document, apply to civil war as well as to international war. This overcomes a weakness in a good deal of the previous law on that matter. Also, it is noteworthy that there are certain supranational elements in many of these developments not evident in much of the earlier law in this field.

This leads us to an area which overlaps with Paddy Ashdown's discussion about intervention, in Chapter 2. In the 1990s, humanitarian issues, and in particular violation of the laws of war, became a basis for military intervention. This was unforeseen by most writers in the field, and it goes flat against the traditional separation of *jus ad bellum* from *jus in bello*. We are all familiar with the notion that these are two separate subjects, as reiterated correctly by Professor Christopher Greenwood.[2] They are conceptually separate but they overlap in numerous ways, the most important of which is the beginning of a justification for intervention on the grounds of violation of the laws of war.

The UN Security Council's response to many conflicts in the 1990s has involved much emphasis on humanitarian norms, humanitarian assistance and observance of international humanitarian law. The word 'humanitarian', which does not appear to have occurred in Security Council resolutions before 1990, has been constantly reiterated in resolutions since that time.

Why has there been this emphasis on humanitarian issues? It has been argued that it is easier for great powers, which cannot agree on substantive solutions to crises, to agree on minor humanitarian, ameliorative resolutions that appear to suggest undertaking some form of action in order to resolve the crisis, but that actually do not address its root causes. There is a natural tendency for multilateral organizations, especially the UN, to go down that route. Yet there is a paradox which has reasserted itself time and time again, at the heart of this lowest common denominator approach. If actors adopt this approach and merely propose some humanitarian response to a crisis, what do they do if that humanitarian response is frustrated or is manifestly inadequate? The actors are committed to

---

[2] Christopher Greenwood, 'International law, just war and the conduct of modern military operations', in P. Mileham and L. Willett (eds), *Ethical Dilemmas of Military Interventions* (London: Royal Institute of International Affairs, 1999).

involvement in the crisis in some form. When that runs into trouble, they need to reassess the situation and formulate stronger decisions. The logic of stressing humanitarian issues itself leads on to humanitarian intervention in its classic sense, the legally precise sense, i.e. military intervention in order to protect the human rights of a state's inhabitants that does not have the authority of its government. There are broader meanings to humanitarian intervention as well, but this is the classic and precise meaning of the term.

It is possible to view in this light the actions of outside powers in a large number of situations in the 1990s. In northern Iraq in 1991, the basis for action was in legal terms almost identical to the basis for action over Kosovo. There was a UN Security Council resolution which willed the end but did not will the means. However, the action by the coalition intervening within northern Iraq was relatively uncontroversial because it was so manifestly tailored to achieve the end in view. Somalia in 1992, Rwanda in 1994, Haiti in 1994 and Kosovo in 1999 are cases in which violations of humanitarian law have been cited by various bodies, including the Security Council, as a basis for intervention.

Despite the frequency of these cases, which indicates a real problem in the international system, it is very difficult to develop and define a coherent doctrine either for the circumstances in which humanitarian intervention is justified or for the organizations which may authorize humanitarian intervention. Also, there is the issue that some states are bitterly opposed to any doctrine of humanitarian intervention: they may tolerate the occasional practice of humanitarian intervention but they will not tolerate a doctrine. The criticism that Kofi Annan has run into in the current UN General Assembly, after publication of his document about protection of civilians in war, is an indication of how controversial the whole area of humanitarian intervention remains. Russia is deeply opposed to it, China is deeply opposed to it and so are many post-colonial states. I would argue that all these states oppose it for quite good reasons. The presumption in international relations has to be a presumption against intervention. The non-intervention rule is the basis of contemporary international relations. Any violations of that rule have to be exceptional. So I see no chance of a general doctrine emerging. One has to be very careful about asserting that humanitarian intervention is now a new international legal norm, because it does not pass either of two tests. First, where is the text that justifies humanitarian intervention in clear terms? Second, how can one say that something is the new customary norm when the practice is highly contested, and never more so than over Kosovo? I was in favour of the Kosovo operation. Obviously, like anybody else, I had criticisms of this or that aspect, but I thought something had to be done. I do not want to be misunderstood on this point. However I do not think that we can cobble from Kosovo a general doctrine of humanitarian intervention. And if a doctrine were assembled, it would have to be very heavily qualified.

I want to mention too one problem about the present state of international humanitarian law. Of real concern – and I shall be blunt about this – is the policy of the United States. Despite the experiences of the Gulf War in 1990–1 and despite the extreme care with which the US armed forces have approached the task of writing manuals of military law and rules of engagement, the United States is not formally a party to most of the major laws of war agreements of recent decades. In particular it is not a party to the 1977 Protocols I and II, the 1995 Laser Protocol, the 1997 Anti-Personnel Mines Convention or the 1998 Statute of the International Criminal Court. When the major military power in the world has become such a long-term critic of elements of the contemporary laws of war, there is a problem that should be addressed. I do not want to exaggerate the problem. Although the United States is not a party to these accords, it takes them a great deal more seriously that many countries which are parties. The reasons for non-participation require understanding, not condemnation. These reasons are more than merely the whims of a single elderly senator. Yet America's non-participation has the potential for causing some degree of confusion when joint operations are the order of the day.

The last point I want to make is that there appears to be a fundamental problem with the way in which the body of the laws of war has been advocated in recent years. This may partly explain the political problems encountered within the United States. The laws of war are moving in a supranational direction, are being applied to civil wars much more than in the past and are beginning to provide justification for intervention of various kinds. Yet their presentation as something above and beyond the world of states, as something that emerges from high-minded bodies in Geneva such as the International Committee of the Red Cross, is a terrible oversimplification. Both supporters and critics have tended to describe the laws in this way. The truth is that this body of law is far older than the first Red Cross convention: international treaties on matters such as treatment of prisoners or neutrality long pre-date that. The first multilateral convention in this area, the first that was open for any state to sign, had nothing to do with Geneva or the Red Cross: it was the 1856 Paris Maritime Agreement. We need to get back to a view of the law – as not only manifesting an overall belief in humanity and in ethical conduct but also being compatible with military necessity and reflecting the interests of states and their armed forces – which has in part been lost in the last decade or two.

4 Handcuffing the military? Military judgment, rules of engagement and public scrutiny

Michael Ignatieff

The title 'handcuffing the military' was chosen by the military and given to me, a civilian. That, it seems to me, is significant. Many military people feel that the ethical restraints imposed on military practice are a form of handcuffs and that we need to restate the extent to which, in a democracy, the military always are and always should be subject to both political and moral restraint. That is not the issue. I think we realize that the threat of force without intention is empty, and that force without legitimacy is vain. Everything I am going to discuss pertains to the ways in which, if you have legitimacy, force can be effective. If you lose legitimacy, force is not effective. So for force to be legitimate, it must be constrained. The difficult issue is, at what point does control of the military, or ethical restraint on military operations become so constraining that you lose military effectiveness and ultimately legitimacy as well? There is a hard place where that occurs, and we have to define where that is. That is how I construe the topic.

It is obvious to all of us that the restraints on the use of military power are getting tougher, getting tighter, and we need to understand why that is the case. Part of the explanation is self-evident. Total wars, wars fought for national survival are not conducted with a very strong degree of ethical restraint. When the *jus ad bellum* is tied into national survival, into absolutely life or death issues, ethical constraints are structured very differently from the way they are in modern campaigns. What has happened now, of course, is that military power, basically since 1945 and particularly since 1989, is no longer linked to national survival or vital national interest, and this factor increases the degree of ethical restraint that must be applied to military power.

My main proposition here is that military risk and military exposure have to be minimized because the political consensus behind the use of

25

military force is shallow. When national survival is at stake, the military can count on the democratic support of the populace to an extreme level. But when military force is used in, say, the attainment of humanitarian objectives or the defence of human rights, the consensus in favour of its use is shallow. The amount of risk you can take, if that is the *jus ad bellum*, is shallow. It means you can use military force provided casualties are low. It means you can use military force, but only up to a certain point. The *jus ad bellum* conditions for going to war are decisively constraining for the type of military operation and force you can use. This sets up a very uncomfortable dynamic for us all, which is that the language which we use to justify military force – human rights, reversing massacre, genocide – is the language of ultimate moral commitment, and it sounds fantastically impressive. It sounds fantastically mobilizing, but what we have discovered is that it mobilizes very little at all. The political consensus behind taking severe military risks in defence of those ultimate objectives is actually shallow. The military are aware of this, and they know that what the public is prepared to support in defence of those objectives is limited.

There are other reasons why the constraints on the military are getting tighter, a principal one being that in the post-Cold War era all armed forces operate among civilians. We do not have battles about civilians 'over here' and civilians 'over there', if we ever did. We have a tremendous dilemma about discrimination: military action among civilians, in the heart of Mogadishu, in the villages of Kosovo, in the villages of Bosnia, requires that discrimination be built into targeting rules.

Another constraint is that we all live in post-imperial democratic cultures. The traditional justification for the use of military power is the acquisition and holding of territory. But in a post-imperial war you do not use military power to acquire territory in perpetuity, and this means that military operations are limited by the logic of an early-exit strategy. This is another important restraint on the use of military power. It derives from the post-imperial principle.

Another factor is technology. This must be emphasized strongly because precision-guided weapons are increasing our capacity to discriminate, and advances in communications are improving command and control. The threshold of precision has been raised; we can be more precise. Because our command and control is better we can demand much more exact manoeuvres and precise behaviour from small troop units. And now that technically commanders have greater control over their units than before and weapon systems are more discriminating, control and discrimination become moral imperatives. This is one aspect of the moving frontier of the Geneva conventions, for example. Military lawyers have said to me that in the future there will be a new type of war crime: you had precision-guided weapons but you did not use them. Once you have a technical capability, you may become obliged to use it. Failure to use it will constitute a crime.

It is particularly important to be aware that constraints on military power do not apply only to soldiers, sailors and airmen. There is a new kind of warrior, the cyber warrior, the information warrior, the man or woman who is waging war in front of a computer console. What rules of war, rules of engagement, rules of restraint are required for them? What are the rules about perfidy? We had a traditional law of war in relation to perfidy – how does that law apply, for example, to the placing on a computer screen of a virtual image of a foreign leader announcing his surrender, as a way of disconcerting the enemy? At what point does information warfare involve us in breaches of the traditional framework of Geneva Convention rules in relation to perfidy and other matters?

New capabilities, a post-imperial context and a sense that military power is no longer legitimated by national survival are some of the elements explaining why the restraints on the use of military power are growing tighter and why military people feel more crowded by ethics than before.

I now want to examine how these restraints are applied in practice on the ground. They are applied through rules of engagement. They are applied right at the place where it gets sharp and difficult – and this place is where young lieutenants on peacekeeping missions have to make these split-second ethical decisions about what to do in dangerous situations. The ethical limits at ground zero are agonizing, and they are the ones I want to discuss.

As a writer who has spent 10 years in the Balkans, Angola and Afghanistan, I am recurrently astonished by the moral dilemmas, the metaphysical weight of the moral dilemmas, placed at very low levels in the chain of command. I owe my life to the fact that a Canadian peacekeeper in Croatia made a particular value choice at a crucial moment. What interests me is how you train people to make these judgment calls in real time, when you have a quarter of a second to do the right thing and a lifetime to live with the wrong thing. The military all know what that is about. We have to talk about training – simulation training, role-playing training. This is much more than teaching the rules, it is getting people somehow to live through these dilemmas on the ground. And as the ethical sharp end is right down at the level of the lieutenant, the sergeant, the corporal, we must also talk about a decentralization of power. We have to talk about shifting the power down. If the moral responsibility is down on the ground, we had better get a command structure that gives the lieutenant, sergeant, corporal the power down there to make these decisions and then the capacity to pass the decision-making responsibility upward again when they need to. In other words, it is not just a matter of training – we may be talking about changing the structure of our armed forces.

We are already doing it in the sense that if you talk to the commandant of the United States Marine Corps, he talks about a 'strategic corporal'. A 'strategic corporal' is not just strategic in the military sense, crucially he is strategic in the ethical sense. He would be at a checkpoint having to make very difficult moral judgments: who is a refugee, who is not a refugee? Who is a combatant, who is a non-combatant? Do I call in fire here or do I call in the local faith healer? These are incredibly tough calls. So the 'strategic corporal' is an ethical as well as a military figure, and we have to figure out forms of training, forms of teaching, forms of role-playing which empower military officers at the front line to make the right moral choices.

We know that the costs of getting a decision wrong are really serious. Bloody Sunday haunts the British army. The story of the British army in Ireland is in some sense the story of how a great army, with a great regimental tradition, overcame the stain of that event – whatever the causes, whatever the blame – and managed, by the skin of its teeth, in my judgment as an outsider, to preserve the legitimacy of British armed power in that part of the United Kingdom. So huge things ride on it making the right moral choice: the honour of regiments, the honour of the army and the credibility of civilian power in holding on to contested provinces. Canada too has lived with this dilemma in huge ways. One stupid mistake in Somalia involving the torture of a civilian helped to destroy the regimental honour of our armed forces for a time. We had to purge ourselves. This has had immense implications for civilian identity. Canada has built its identity for 30 or 40 years on the idea of 'we're the good guys, we're never going to stiff somebody'. We did kill somebody in Somalia, and we have had to dig ourselves out ever since.

I have a book called *Hard Choices*. It has General Romeo Dallaire's absolutely heartrending description of being the Canadian commander of the UNAMIR (United Nations Assistance Mission in Rwanda) contingent. I advise you to go out and read it immediately. It is an account of when an operation goes wrong, of what going wrong really looks like. The consequences for him personally, the consequences for the armed forces, have been horrendous. So I am saying, let us exercise discipline by a firm awareness of what happens when an operation goes wrong; when you get the conditions for the legitimate use of force wrong; when you have the wrong chain of command, as was the case with UNAMIR; when the forces do not have the back-up; and when the mission is unclear. You put young men in danger in a way that has consequences for the whole operation, and this means that when military power itself is dishonoured and shamed, the consequences are extremely serious.

Those were problems on the ground. Now I turn to air power. I shall not dwell much on the Jakobitzi bridge bombing itself. That was the most serious moral or ethical problem in the Kosovo war concerning the use of force, and it decisively and instantly affected the legitimacy of the whole campaign. This is why our subject is such a serious business. A pilot pulls the trigger at 15,000 feet and makes a perfectly understandable, even legitimate mistake, but the repercussions of that mistake in the age of instant communication can actually destroy the political legitimacy of an entire military operation. A passenger train was hit and there were civilian casualties. That is why those at the sharp end now bear such a huge moral responsibility, because the moral responsibility is simultaneously a political responsibility. A pilot's error can potentially jeopardize a whole military campaign. In my judgment this is surely a new historical fact in the history of warfare.

I have given a sense of what the consequences of a military mistake are. One result of everybody's heightened awareness of the consequences has been to bring the lawyers in. This is a huge fact in the history of warfare. I have read recently *The Air Lawyers*, the history of the United States Judge Advocate General's Office. My understanding of the history of American air lawyers is that in 1965 they were not allowed near a targeting cell. Throughout the whole Vietnam campaign there was not a lawyer within 100 yards of anybody who was doing serious business in the air. A change in this approach appears to have come about by the time of the US invasion of Panama, when there was a much closer involvement in the whole operation. In 1991 General Norman Schwarzkopf involved lawyers extensively in the conduct of the Gulf War: the assessment of targets was made with lawyers, the whole prisoner exchange operation was done with lawyers. General Schwarzkopf is publicly quoted as saying that 'this was the most legal war ever fought in the history of the American armed forces'. In 1999, when I did some reporting on the conduct of the air campaign in Kosovo, I discovered that the Judge Advocate's Office at EUCOM, Central European Command, had lawyers who were plugged in by computer in real time for the whole assemblage of each target folder. The lawyers sat there, and the 'weaponeers' would do their job and the 'targeteers' would do their job. Then the lawyer would assess on a computer screen what were the collateral damage implications, and the Geneva Convention implications, for each and every target. This is a new factor in the history of warfare. I think it is going to continue. I think it is a good thing, but let us also be clear that, as I understand, it caused certain missions to be cancelled in mid-air.

The other point that needs to be pressed home very clearly is that allies, people with common legal traditions, common understandings and common goals, often construe the rules differently. My understanding of the conduct of the air campaign in Kosovo is that the Americans thought that the television station tower was an acceptable military target. The British, I gather, did not. The Americans thought that hitting a power grid was just inside the Geneva Conventions and an acceptable military target. The British felt there were too many dual-use implications and did not agree. So in literal terms, the British did not fly those missions and the Americans did. Clearly, the fact that two national cultures, with the same legal tradition and the same culture can construe the same thing very differently has huge alliance implications in military ethics. I am sure those differences translate out in troop deployments on the ground in Kosovo. The Americans will have one set of rules of engagement for many situations, the British will have other ones. I am talking about micro-ethics here: about how you judge, how you make the call second by second in real time. Many judgments rest on the shoulders of young platoon leaders in each national culture, and they are making different calls. We need to have a better sociology of how they are making these calls differently, in order to help them make better judgments. The front-line leaders do a superb job. I could not make some of the calls they make, and I am the beneficiary of some of those calls, so I am not making a pious civilian critique of their military judgment. I want to support the soldiers at the front line, not criticize them negatively.

In working towards a conclusion, let me revert to my original question – are the handcuffs on the military now too tight? We have lawyers involved in every decision and we have very tight rules of engagement, both of which reflect the tightening ethical restraints on the use of military power that I have discussed. As a result, I see one basic problem: we seem to be playing by rules but the other side does not. This has real, explosive consequences. The NATO countries are Geneva Convention armies; they are fighting people who are not Geneva Convention armies. Sometimes this happens, as in Somalia, because the other side consists of the tribesmen, ultimate paramilitaries, and of non-regular units, teenage thugs, kids, bandits – the Mogadishu scenario. Sometimes – and this is where ethical decisions get tough – the other side knows that we play by the Geneva Convention rules and exploits the fact that we do. This is a huge ethical dilemma for us. They put their tanks and command posts near the civilians. This happened in Kosovo; the Serbs were exploiting our observance of the Geneva Convention rules.

That poses dilemma number one for us. Do we decide to call their bluff and strike close and risk civilian casualties so that they will not play this Geneva Convention double bluff with us?

Dilemma number two is that the moral standard we have set renders us vulnerable to our own domestic opinion in terms of zero casualties and asymmetries of risk. Knowing that we seek to minimize collateral damage, opponents exploit through the media any mistake we make. Our obser-vance of ethical restraints makes us more vulnerable to media war. If we hit a train, because in real time the pilot cannot stop pulling the trigger as it comes into the sights or if we hit a convoy because there is a military target at its head, they have cameras on the ground broadcasting our mistake to the whole world. Our ethical vulnerability to this reproach is then exploited by the enemy in order to challenge our will to continue combat. It is a direct blow at the legitimacy of the conditions for the use of force. That is the essential point. This is war. When they put the CNN cameras on the Jakobitzi road, this is war because they are attempting to get at our civilian opinion-formers, saying that this war has become illegitimate. That is possible only because we are playing by the rules. We have set a moral standard, which then renders us vulnerable in relation to our own domestic opinion.

The most obvious and most visible rule is the 'zero casualty' rule we have set for our own forces, and there is a real moral tension between force protection and force effectiveness. Force protection has become the chief moral imperative governing the use of military force. This becomes self-defeating. If you are going to go in, you have to make it clear to the enemy that you are prepared to take casualties, otherwise he does not believe your force is credible. The big ticket question here, in other words, is whether the ethical constraints that we have imposed on our armed forces are eroding the credibility of our military deterrent itself. We are in a situation in which it might not even have been enough to amass 175,000 troops on the borders of Kosovo in Albania and Macedonia because Milosevic would still have calculated we were not prepared to act. The fact that our ethical restraints may be compromising the credibility of our deterrent means we would have to prove that credibility beyond doubt the hard, nasty and rough way. Perversely, restraint may make us more ruthless in the end.

I wish, finally, to reassert my fundamental point, which is to get us away from the big philosophical discussions about *jus ad bellum* and *jus in bello*, and down to a very practical question: how can we enable the 'strategic' corporal and the pilot to manage ethical problems effectively as well as to be militarily effective? As I have said, this issue has enormous political consequences. I have no experience of military training. Many of you do. I simply want to put this question on the table because, as I said at the start, force without legitimacy is vain. We have to get the balance between force and legitimacy right so that our concern for legitimacy does not cancel out the credibility and utility of force itself. That is our dilemma. We then have to turn the sense of that dilemma into operational guidelines for our men and women at ground zero. We leave them to make the decisions that we, in the tranquillity of a beautiful setting such as Sandhurst, can talk about but that they have to make at the point of a gun.

5 Kosovo: its ethical implications

James P. McCarthy

My judgment is that NATO faced in its campaign in Kosovo against Serbian forces a number of ethical issues that it could have controlled but did not. Thus it acted in an unethical and possibly immoral manner. Before defending this judgment, I must point out that NATO has set the standard in the West of armed forces conducting perfect military operations. Although I am critical of a number of areas, my overall assessment is that the Kosovo campaign was executed very effectively. Professional military people can be very proud of what they accomplished, even though my focus is going to be on their mistakes.

NATO's decision to intervene had the traditional arguments for and against. Intervention would stop the genocide and the mass destruction of property. It had the tacit consent of important sections of the international community, as it seemed to meet the just war criteria of those who advocated it. There was some legal precedent for it, and, in fact, many people argued that there was a moral obligation to intervene. The arguments against intervention have been well covered at this conference. Regarding the state sovereignty issue, some lawyers would argue that there is no specific basis in international law for intervention. But there is a long precedent of non-intervention and we are not intervening elsewhere in circumstances that may be even more horrible than in Kosovo.

In this presentation I accept, having previously diagnosed it, that there might have been a moral reason to intervene in Kosovo. Then I go into the details of my assessment of NATO's actions. My thesis, based on a preliminary analysis, is that NATO's political and military actions leading up to and during the Kosovo operation, were inconsistent with just war principles and lawful conduct in war in three primary areas. First, military intervention is the last resort. Second, the application of power in an incremental or proportional approach was less effective. Third, the specific rules of engagement (RoE) seemed to be inconsistent in their application. An advocate of least intervention, recalling some of the tenets of just war theory – just cause, wider intention, prospects of success and legitimate authority – would judge they all were met. So it is on last resort and proportionality that I intend to focus my presentation.

Last resort

The revolution in military affairs has had a significant impact on the decision-making process. It has given NATO and my country, the United States, an increased number of alternative courses of action. Unfortunately, the military options are better developed and appear more practicable than diplomatic or economic options. Technological enhancements, particularly of US forces, make it appear as though there can be a quick and clean skirmish. That expectation, supported by a stand-off weapons capability, the lethality of small units, and also precision strikes, increases the military options and the forces that may be selected. Further, the United States has more time to select a military course of action because its forces have been equipped and trained for very rapid deployment.

On the other hand, the additional time for making decisions may not be used effectively because it also increases the time for vacillation. This time should be spent on clarifying objectives and assessing whether the planned course of action is capable of meeting those objectives. My argument is that in Kosovo, NATO did not do that.

In Kosovo, NATO entrapped itself in a policy box. Its threats to use force to achieve a negotiated settlement with Slobodan Milosevic created a box with no way out, when he declined to accept its terms. Totally focused on using military threats to achieve its objective, NATO failed to use the other tools of statecraft which might have prevented the war. This led to a major miscalculation. NATO was so convinced that Milosevic would capitulate that it was unprepared to conduct sustained combat operations. Political leaders were so positive about the apparent success of Rambouillet in deterring the Belgrade leadership from acting against the Albanian population in Kosovo that military leaders were not permitted to and did not plan a major military campaign. As a matter of fact, when operations began, only 51 targets had been selected for the campaign, and the expectation was that this operation would be completed in two days. When that failed to happen, there was certainty that it would be completed in 10 days, which proved to be an underestimation. Finally, there was recognition that this was going to be a relatively long war if NATO continued to fight it the way it was supposed to do, with the overwhelming impact of airpower.

Milosevic, however, was so convinced that NATO would never agree on combat operations that he attempted to call its bluff. NATO's sending of such mixed signals, particularly with its statement of no ground forces, conveyed an apparent lack of will to Milosevic that caused his miscalculation. There was further miscalculation on both sides that led to an ill-timed initiation of the war and then to prolonged combat operations. More loss of life and physical damage resulted and seriously affected the lives of most Serbs living in Kosovo.

What were the consequences of this policy box and its miscalculation? The set of political circumstances created in the beginning precluded NATO from taking any other action, because that would have been judged by the public on both sides as a lack of resolve. This ill-conceived political approach, as I have noted above, then placed the military in an early position of not having a strategy, of not having a military campaign plan about which there was a consensus among the NATO countries. In consequence, NATO, with 570 million people and 56 per cent of the world's Gross National Product (GNP), took on a nation of 22 million people with less than one per cent of the global GNP. It used a significant amount of power, including 38,000 aircraft sorties, 820 aircraft, more than 300 cruise missiles and 23,000 bombs. It took disproportionate means and 78 days to achieve very limited military objectives. In my view that is an ethical and moral issue.

Proportionality

NATO had no political and military agreement on how to fight. It lacked a strategy. The use particularly of ground forces was restricted and there was no agreement on targeting, all of which increased the limitations on the fighting of the conflict as it progressed. These circumstances led to political actions designed to show NATO's solidarity, because it communicated a lack of solidarity and momentum, which I shall describe below. This perceived lack of solidarity had significant consequences for the Serbian people and it highlighted a difference in perceptions of proportionality. Views on the right strategy diverged. To summarize a very complex issue, many airmen believed that the way to bring this conflict to a conclusion was to strike at the heart of Serbia and its military capability, as well as those other targets that would provide diminishing political support for Milosevic. Others, however, were attracted to what was happening in Kosovo and tried to stop the ethnic cleansing from the air, in the worst weather conditions experienced in the Balkans probably for a century and with an adversary who was very astute. This placed NATO's air forces in a very difficult position which was made more difficult by the fact that even the military leaders could not agree on the proper strategy for conducting this operation. The public announcement of no ground forces gave Milosevic important courses of action that enabled his forces to operate and survive and significantly increased NATO's task. This policy judgment was carried to an extreme, in that the Supreme Allied Commander Europe (SACEUR) was not permitted to establish a ground component commander to advise him on how to conduct operations against Serbian forces in Kosovo, lest the public judge NATO was going to use ground forces in the first place.

In my judgment, proportionality works two ways. We all understand that too much force can be applied, force that would be disproportionate to accomplishing the objective. I would make the argument, however, that too little force, or that which is improperly applied – particularly with significant political limits to maintain a consensus of the publics of the NATO countries – increases the destruction and increases the casualties. It is very difficult to judge how to analyse this outcome but I believe that the combined actions prolonged the war and will make our efforts to rebuild – when we eventually take on that responsibility – very, very difficult.

On escalation, the lesson the United States learned in Vietnam was that slowly increased application of military power prolongs conflict and increases the damage not only to people but also to the infrastructure of a country. Further, it actually stiffens resolve over time, because a nation can adjust to a gradual worsening of conditions. This has the effect of prolonging the war and increasing the damage.

Let me mention briefly the matter of target selection. NATO target lists were developed from an analysis of effects-based warfare. We have developed a capability in the United States – there is a similar capability in a number of NATO nations – to understand a target fully. That is, if you wish to nullify a communications system, there are the key nodes that can be destroyed which permit fairly easy restoration immediately after the conflict. To draw upon an experience from the Iraqi conflict in taking down an oil refinery – unlike what the Allies did in the Second World War when they dropped dumb bombs all over and totally destroyed a facility – we learned that in the southeastern corner of a certain building there was a set of controls. If these controls were destroyed, the entire operation could be shut down. The amount of damage done to the facility would be one or two per cent, but the facility would remain non-operational until new controls could be procured from the West and installed.

In this level of detail lies the significance of this new targeting concept. Yet because the NATO target-approval process in effect permitted any country to withdraw a target from the list, the resulting target sets were relatively ineffective. While military leaders respect the right of states and political leaders to establish the parameters for military operations, and their rationale for doing so, the consequences of political withholding of individual targets is significant: operational effectiveness is reduced and the requirement to kill more targets to achieve the desired effect is increased.

NATO's military compromises, in effect, went counter to its political objective, which was to shorten the war and minimize the damage. There were other operational consequences too. For example – and worse from an aviator's standpoint – the delay in the decision-making process affected the operational cycle. Some withholds of targets were decided so late that the aircrew had already started engines before they were notified of the cancellation. As a result, a formation that depended on mutual support from a full complement was actually denied that support because each day a number of aircraft did not launch.

Finally, momentum. Because Slobodan Milosevic failed to capitulate in the early days of the war, the NATO leaders saw the need to build momentum, for example by deploying more combat aircraft than were needed and increasing the number of targets struck each day. The result was more risk to NATO forces and increased damage to Serbia. So we

37

dropped 23,000 bombs, and only 22 are judged to have created any collateral damage in our initial assessment. Obviously, we were less effective and less successful than we could have been if we had properly applied military force in the beginning.

Maintaining the high moral ground

My third and final point is much more difficult to articulate: it is about maintaining the moral high ground. In some ways Milosevic won the information war, in that he was able to make NATO forces appear ineffective and to undermine their legitimacy. I think that the military should always be accountable for its actions, both during and following an operation, and the media provide an important role in that accountability. So I am not arguing against that. But let me give you examples.

The Serbs made the issue of casualties a matter of huge moral consequence – in effect, a new centre of gravity. 'Centres of gravity' is a military term that denotes the focal points for the energies of a military force. When the air campaign started – and it started because NATO intelligence indicated that Milosevic was going to send his forces into Kosovo in a very large effort, which he did – NATO/US JSTARS (Joint Surveillance, Targeting, Acquisition and Reconnaissance System) watched those tactical formations moving in, and they made very lucrative targets. As soon as NATO reacted, Milosevic dispersed his forces very effectively so that the ethnic cleansing in Kosovo was done at the company or platoon level rather than by a larger tactical formation. Not only that, he dispersed his forces among the civilians, and interspersed his convoys with civilian vehicles; in many cases, he commandeered civilian vehicles to move his supplies and equipment. This made the task of trying to disrupt ethnic cleansing from the air very difficult. Moreover, the Serbs positioned their forces very close to schools, hospitals and mosques. When I was in Kosovo looking at targets that had been destroyed, there was a tank sitting right up against the wall of a hospital. The tank was positioned within a foot of that wall, so that if NATO forces took out the tank, which was successfully done with a laser-guided munition, there was a high probability that they would hit the wall and possibly the hospital. Also, some have suggested that for the first two weeks of the war the Serbs had access to the air tasking order that identified targets and times of attack. Further, there is established evidence that the Serbs took civilians, put them into these target areas and locked the doors knowing that within a relatively short period of time a NATO weapon would destroy it and the people in it. Then they were quick to drag the press over to observe these casualties.

NATO faced a dilemma. It sought to minimize collateral damage, specifically civilian casualties but in doing so it encouraged Milosevic to continue to put civilians close to targets. How should one handle that moral dilemma? Let me relate what happened in terms of various operations. Fighter pilots need to know what the target is; they need to know the rules of engagement. As avoiding collateral damage, particularly these civilian centres of gravity became very important, the fighter pilot, flying at approximately 700 miles an hour, was now not only required to find the target and destroy it within the few seconds available. He also had to look at the target, judge that the ordnance was correct and that he would hit the target and then judge that there would be no collateral damage – no civilians or military, other than those in the tank or the surface-to-air missile site, who would be killed or injured. To the fighter pilots' credit, a number of them returned to their bases saying, 'I could not make all those judgments'. This restriction also had the effect of requiring eyes on targets either through an electro-optical sensor such as the *Predator* or *Hunter* unmanned aerial vehicle or someone in another aircraft who would assess the effects and radio back to the other pilots that it was a reasonable target. That action introduced a significant risk into the operation.

The altitude restriction on NATO air operations of 15,000 feet was intended to minimize the risk to them. But after Milosovic interspersed his forces among the civilian population it was impossible to distinguish between convoys from any height. Therefore we stopped attacking them.

My own experience of 152 combat missions in the Vietnam War was that I was never bound by so many conditions. I felt I followed an ethical course in terms of minimizing civilian casualties and collateral damage in the context of that war.

In relation to the bombing of the television tower in central Belgrade, the commander, recognizing the rules of engagement, said, 'OK, I have got to take down this tower, and I cannot affect the top floor that has civilians working on it.' Whether or not they should have struck at the tower is certainly another issue, but how do you otherwise take it down? A 2,000-pound bomb would have taken it down in a moment, but with much collateral damage. So the military asked for the high explosive to be removed from bombs so that they could be dropped with concrete in them as a way to take the tower down. Through kinetic energy, this would have worked very effectively. However, it would have been several weeks before the bombs were ready. So a tactical cruise missile was used. It approached from a precise direction and at a certain precise altitude, hit the tower, knocked it down and avoided collateral damage. That was a fairly difficult way to kill a target, but it still worked. As a result commanders asked for smaller and smaller weapons because the precision permits you to destroy a target and minimizes collateral damage.

Now I would like to discuss a moral dilemma concerning the conduct of war in the information age and to have a candid discussion of the issues. I shall give one example. SACEUR used a video teleconference (VTC) as a way to conduct his operations. He used it at least daily, sometimes two or three times a day, sometimes for two or three hours, and went all the way down to wing commander level on television. The good part was that there was no question about guidance: everyone permitted to attend the VTC understood all the issues that were being discussed. For a method of communicating downward, it was wonderful. But there is a different problem. First, the amount of time spent on VTC is time that cannot be spent on other responsibilities. The second difficulty is, what officer – wing commander, colonel or brigadier general – is willing to criticize SACEUR when there are three, four or five intermediate levels of command that will hear this criticism? Even the Joint Task Force commander, a Navy admiral, said that in front of all those subordinate commanders he was not going to criticize the actions of SACEUR. Military protocol or reticence impedes, if not blocks, the normal processes by which subordinates communicate opposing or divergent opinions. I find from my inquiries that this problem was never resolved. We must learn how to deal with the new methods of communication.

What is my general conclusion and solution? NATO had a just cause, the right intention, a good prospect for success and legitimate authority. All that is good, but I would argue that in last resort and proportionality NATO failed to meet the principles of just war. It was not because people were immoral; it was because the issues were complex and we have not yet learned how to grapple with them effectively.

What can be done? I think that preliminary findings coming from the Kosovo war need to be considered in an ethical context. We need to broaden the moral and ethical discussion and bring it to a more practical level. What are the dilemmas and how are they best dealt with? The VTC, for example, probably was never considered from an ethical or moral standpoint. It has other problems as well, but we need to consider it from that standpoint. I think most military leaders *do* consider the just war theory or other beliefs. We need to broaden that understanding, and our education; we need to discuss these issues, and some that I have presented warrant statistical analysis. For example, does a prolonged and escalated approach indeed cause more damage than forceful and quick action taken at the onset? I think the answer is yes, but statistical analysis would give a more precise understanding. Finally, although we talk about educating our military leaders, I consider that the principal problem in Kosovo was policy leadership. How we educate policy-makers about the implications of their political constraints is certainly a difficult challenge.

6 Building force and unit morale and motivation (I)

Rupert Smith

This chapter summarizes my views on building force and unit morale and motivation. I shall not produce detailed arguments to support my assertions, my intention being to provide an agenda for discussion.

I start with a definition. Morale is that spirit held individually or collectively which triumphs in adversity, that spirit which is the motivating will to win when more material motivators are put at nought by circumstances. I do not think its basis needs to be 'ethical' in any sense, other than the ethos of the particular group in question at the time.

The commander of an intervention operation usually finds himself

- with an international force. Each state has sent a contingent to serve its national interest and this interest is reflected in the nature of the contingent and the risks it is permitted to run. To a greater or lesser extent each contingent is different – different language, equipment, training, law, culture etc.
- supporting or cooperating closely with other organizations, such as the United Nations itself and the United Nations High Commissioner for Refugees, all of which have different objectives, cultures, operating methods and so on.
- attempting to achieve an overall objective which is often ill-defined or not defined at all. The military are expected to establish conditions in which the objective can be achieved, but in such a way that they cannot be accused of being partial.
- under the direction of a political body that represents the consensus of its members' interest but that is not necessarily responsible for the political activity of the intervention (NATO and the UN in Kosovo, for example). This body seeks to control and thereby limit risk – the rules of engagement are a case in point. At the same time, each

national contingent answers to its own capital, which frequently has differing views – legal interpretations being an example.

What does the commander do?

- He recognizes reality and works to establish in national capitals a common perception and understanding of what he is doing. The ideal is that capitals are confident of his judgment and that he is not careless of their interest. If he cannot achieve this, capitals will tend to second-guess his decisions.
- He sets the direction and goals, the 'aim', for his command and shows his commanders the 'way' to get there. This is difficult to do at the best of times. The multinational nature of the command and the need to deal with the capitals make for much complexity and friction, which are intensified if other agencies are included.

Now the commander can have all the bright ideas he likes, but he must carry his subordinates with him. They must have such confidence in him that they consent to be led by him and to represent him to advantage to the national capitals. The national commanders are the international commander's best advocate in their capitals. In my view he must concentrate on leading his contingent commanders rather than his command as a whole. It is through them that he will lead his forces. I know it is a counsel of perfection, but he should seek to achieve among these leaders a sense of unity of purpose which, particularly in an intervention for humanitarian ends, amounts to an ethos, a shared recognition of what is to be achieved and the moral limits within which actions are taken towards this end. Unless these commanders understand similarly concepts such as impartiality and proportionality in the particular circumstances of the intervention in question, the morale of the force will suffer.

Once the commander has achieved this goal, or is on the way to doing so, his force will start to operate as a single force as opposed to a collection of forces. To do this requires an understanding of the national military cultures and the societies from which the force is drawn. For example, where in a military hierarchy does the authority to make decisions lie? Does that force respond best to orders or directives? What is it good at and what are its weaknesses? How aggressive is it? With this understanding he can play on the strength of each contingent and appeal to national pride – armies like to be thought well of, and to win. Countries are shamed when their armies do badly. The ideal is to build self-respect and self-confidence by allocating, ordering and supervising missions and tasks in a way appropriate to the contingent. Remember, few of the contingent commanders or men will have experience of the specific circumstances of the operation, and those who have will probably have been promoted to positions in which their experience is not directly relevant. They will have been trained, but the application of their training in the circumstances of the operation will require adventurous decision-making and a comprehension of the operation overall at very low levels in the military hierarchy – it is the corporals and the captains who win these operations. Again, it is another counsel of perfection, but one is seeking to achieve a situation in which, faced with some disaster or other, junior commanders of all contingents can take actions which are appropriate and explicable to the force, to the ever present non-governmental organizations and to the world's press. If this situation is approached, the force feels good about itself, the countries feel good about the force and the force advances towards the objective. States become less risk-adverse.

Good morale brings me to discipline, ideally self-discipline – the spirit that holds a man or men together in the face of fear and adversity. I hold that you cannot have high morale without discipline as I have just defined it. In international forces the enforcement of discipline, like leadership, rests with the national commander. You have to work through these commanders to achieve two things:

- Security of the person, of *matériel* and of information. International operations regularly take place among the mass of the population. Discipline must be such that individual soldiers and small units conduct themselves correctly among them. The need for personal security is self-evident, but this is not the case with *matériel* or information, particularly when these are the property of the 'Alliance' or 'International Community' rather than a specific country. One measure of the discipline of the force as a whole is the readiness of the members of each national component to secure what is of interest to the whole force. Put another way, the frequency of black market dealings or the leakage of information, either about operations or interpersonal and interstate tensions, is a direct indication of ill-discipline. Operating in larger groups, or to a rigid plan by centralizing decisions and thus ensuring supervision, tends to be ineffective because of the national element and impracticalities. It is especially essential for international operations that effective decisions appropriate to the circumstances are made in time to be effective at a low level in the hierarchy of command.

- To advance the enterprise, that is to take appropriate action to move towards the desired objective. This requires commanders at all levels to act positively. To do so requires in turn a comprehension of the operation, its geography, its socio-economic and political factors or, for the junior commander, the 'pattern of life', and his part in achieving the desired outcome. He must understand the law and the consequences of his action. Above all, he must have the discipline to take appropriate action, unsupervised and without reference to his superiors. It is in the here and now of crisis and battle that ethics becomes critical. The junior commander must have an understanding of right and wrong and act to prevent wrong. It will be too late if he does not act: the wrong will multiply. The consequence of junior commanders failing to take action to advance towards the objective is at best stasis, and at worst a loss of initiative. The loss of the moral initiative in operations for essentially moral objectives among civilians, whether in the theatre of combat or in front of the TV at home, is dangerous. When something has gone wrong, particularly in the face of the tendency for comment or judgment to be issued along with fact in reporting, commanders at all levels need to present a good story, one that stands moral scrutiny – yet another counsel of perfection! The measures to achieve this standard of discipline and the degree to which it is achieved will to a large extent reflect the nature of the army and society from which the contingent is drawn. The international commander must understand this and work towards high discipline through the contingent commander. Once again, the commander must understand the nature of the components of his command.

In sum, when in command of an international force conducting an intervention mission, one should seek to establish:

- a common perception of the situation with national capitals, both directly and through the commander of each nation's contingent.
- a measure of confidence on the part of the capitals and the directing political body in the commander's judgment and in the way he intends to reach the intended objective.
- leadership of the contingent commanders, through whom he leads and directs his force, and, through them, the devolution of decision-making authority to junior commanders, whenever possible.
- discipline within the force, in particular the discipline to act to advance towards the objective.

A commander must recognize at all times that this is not a perfect world, otherwise his command would not be required to conduct the operation in the first place.

7 Building force and unit morale and motivation (II)

Loup Francart

Everyone has experienced moments of contingency, moments when the situation was dangerous, the stress was intense and a decision had to be made rapidly. This is as valid in a military context as it is in other professional, or even family and social, contexts. There are several sorts of response to this type of situation: paralysis and hysteria or calmness and effectiveness. Why are there several sorts of response? Does it all depend on personality, education and training in the face of the unexpected? The answer is not that simple. It depends on situations, on the dilemmas and on the expectations of others. It seems impossible to make a rational analysis which would give us the criterion for the 'appropriate reaction'. What seems obvious is that at a given stage, the behaviour of the person will change. He or she may refuse to become involved or may seek actively to address the situation. The latter is significant for us, as we expect each serviceman to commit himself fully in theatres of operation.

What we are looking for is the ability to face the unexpected contingency and to deal with stress. This ability results not only from behaviour but also from an attitude and a way of thinking. Military commitments do not require only know-how. They demand initiative and a will to act in a chaotic environment. This is true for an entire force at each echelon.

There are three major issues linked with this topic. At the level of the military force as a whole, there is the issue of the legitimacy of the military action. This should not be confused with that of the political legality of the commitment. It constitutes a new issue in comparison to our conception of commitments in the context of the Cold War. At the level of tactical units (battalions, companies), the issue of rules of engagement (RoE) is important. The RoE must constitute guidelines for the action. Lastly, at the officer, NCO and private soldier level, the issues of morale and the ability to face a contingency are significant.

Figure 7.1: The sense of the use of force

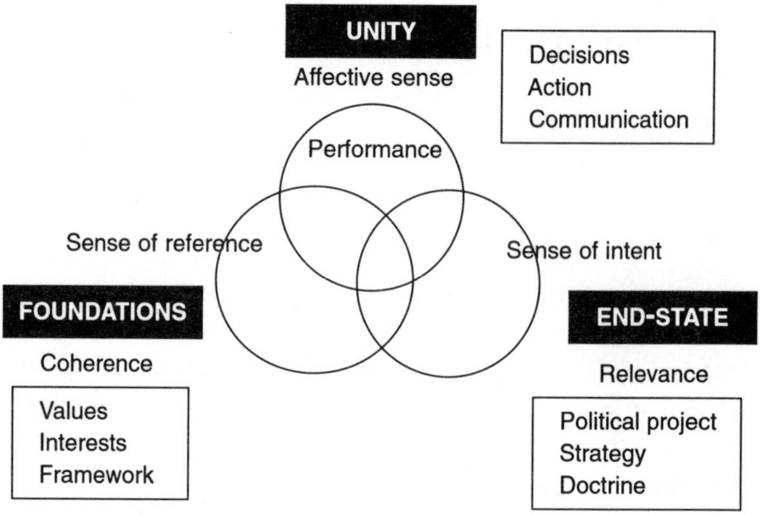

Before dealing with these three points, let me mention a few aspects of current military commitments that influence morale and actions and that must be addressed within the framework of military ethics.

- The political end state. This is complex and not always clearly defined.
- The life of civilians, their suffering and the effects of this suffering on the morale of our troops. Thinking may be replaced by emotion.
- Facing belligerents who are not declared enemies complicates the decision-making process.
- The political impact of a tactical error in a media environment risks the paralysis of reactions.

At the level of the overall force, the purpose of the military intervention must be stressed. In the new millennium, the use of force must make sense. The question is not just that of the philosophical meaning of life but that of the action itself. The two are closely linked: without a meaning in life, there is no action – only a reaction for survival – and without a meaning in the action, life has no meaning. The notion of the sense and purpose of the use of force must be understood in its different aspects, which are indicated in Figure 7.1.

- Logical sense or significance. It constitutes the *sense of reference* which gives coherence to the action to reach a desired 'end-state'.
- Sense as a direction. It is the *intentional sense* which makes action relevant or not.
- Sense, as in sensible and sensitive. It is the *affective sense*, the feeling for an action in a specific context, which determines its performance.

The circumstances or foundations of the military commitment constitute major factors conditioning and giving coherence to the action and the command of operations. They also constitute the dilemmas of military action in the new strategic context of intervention. These foundations are values, interests and frameworks (rules), which set limits.

Values (Box 7.1) signify the true dignity, value and richness of human beings. Having values marks the difference between the actions of humans and those of animals. Values constitute cultural foundations. However, the fact that the same values are not shared by all is one of the problems facing current military commitments.

Interests (Box 7.2) constitute the second set of circumstances or foundations of military action. Interests may be close to values but they have different origins, including the will to survive, defence of the territory, protection of advantages obtained and extension of influence. The notion of interest, on which all defence policies are based, must now be redefined in our current context (see Box 7.2). Ideally, there should be unity in all these interests, but that is not always the case. The frameworks of action are composed of rules set by laws and institutions. I shall deal with this issue in the second part of this chapter.

The aims of military commitments centre on three questions. What political aim guides the military decision to intervene? What is the most appropriate military strategy? What doctrine for force employment will be implemented? These questions require much thought. At the political level, there needs to be a common understanding of the extent and nature of the commitment. This is more important now because many such commitments are met by multinational forces. This issue was evident during

Box 7.1: Values

- **Moral values**
  Love/truth/goodness/beauty

- **Humanitarian values**
  Human rights/justice/solidarity/responsibility/tolerance/respect for others/health

- **Community values**
  Respect for civilizations and cultures/common history/common territory/equality of races and ethnic groups

- **International values**
  Nationhood and sovereignty/rights of populations

- **Social and political values**
  Law/public order/justice/progress/liberty/democracy/pluralism

the air campaign over Yugoslavia. The question is whether Europe could and should have a united position. This is the problem we shall have to solve in the coming decade.

At the military level, the question of the strategic choices for the employment of force is crucial. Do we want a military victory or do we want to restore peace without entering into conflict with an adversary? Do we want to conduct war or do we want to avoid it? On the back of these issues, there is a tendency among involved nations to develop an *ad hoc* doctrine that enables the imposition of the national and international will by force, if deemed necessary, and the prevention, containment and control of violence in-theatre without entering into conflict.

The issue of morale and the legitimacy of commitment are based not only on values, interests and rules and on aims but also on reality. Reality may be defined as what has happened or is happening. Reality raises the issue of command at all levels. There are several points to note in this context:

- Unity of conception, action and communication at each level of force. Decisions must not be contradictory. This is difficult to

Box 7.2 Interests

- **World interests**
  Non-proliferation of nuclear weapons/prevention of and protection against global nuclear, biological and chemical pollution/ protection of water sources and biosphere and prevention of contagious diseases

- **Western interests**
  World stability/European stability/free movement in international zones/nuclear non-proliferation/counter-terrorism

- **National interests**
  Defence of national territory/defence of citizens

- **National strategic interests**
  Energy supply/routes for circulation for goods and citizens/travel/ vital information/alliances and agreements

- **National interests of power**
  Commercial interests/agricultural interests/industrial interests/ financial interests/scientific and technological interests/cultural interests

achieve in a multinational context, in which there are often two chains of command (national and international), whether or not there should be.

- Relevance of actions, also vital. This must stem from a common understanding of the action. This common understanding exists only among a few Western countries.
- Communication and unity of language. These are significant when difficulty in giving meaning to the military commitment leads to a 'war of meaning' in the media.

Our reasoning must go further along this path. In the Cold War, such questions were not asked. The defence of vital Western interests created an automatic consensus between governments, military commanders and civilian populations. Today, such a consensus is not automatic. Rules must be set and frameworks for military action developed.

The commitment of military forces in a chaotic situation, in which there is no enemy but only hostile elements, requires that precise rules must be given to the military force involved. These rules must be applied to differentiate the employment of 'armed force' and the use of 'violence'. Often journalists say that we use violence. This is not so: we are employed to use military 'force'. This distinction may seem trivial to many but it is essential in the current strategic context.

What is force? Force is the power of physical and moral energy. It is the capacity to constrain through action. Force can be measured with regard to the effects it can have. Only its violent application can be criticized or blamed. The term 'violence' comes from the Latin term *violentia*, which means an excess of force. It is also linked with the term *violare*, to violate or act against. The Greek notion of excess, *hubris*, means abuse of power.

Having rules so as to avoid descending into violence is essential. We do not act to survive any more but to protect, to restore and to impose peace. These objectives cannot be achieved through the same type of force as we used in order to defend our vital interests. Moreover, as we may intervene alongside other countries, it is vital for common rules to be established so that the whole force acts in uniformity and that some national forces are prevented from descending into violence.

Several factors must be taken into account in distinguishing between force and violence. First, it is important to know what is the motivation of the action in question. Second, it is necessary to know the geopolitical point of application of force. Courses of action must also be adapted to the goals and points of application. Lastly, the intensity of the force must be measured. The law of armed conflict is based on these significant distinctions between force and violence.

At a less philosophical level, three frameworks define the limits of the legitimate use of force (see Figure 7.2). The legal framework is defined by national and international law. Armed forces have to respect both of these. The international mandate given to the international force is an additional part of the legal framework. The international mandate gives the action its legitimacy. The institutional framework defines military legitimacy. Military legitimacy stems from political legitimacy and sets the rules for the employment of forces. The ethical framework depends on the discernment of each commander. It is based on the respect of human

Figure 7.2: Limits of use of military force

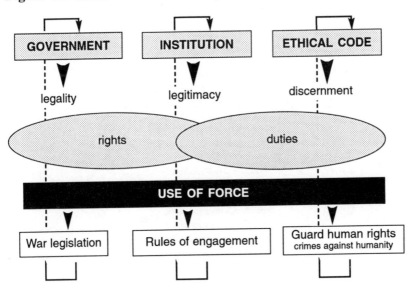

rights and the notion of crime against humanity (UN Resolution 177, 1947). It includes the capacity to distinguish between right and wrong.

Rules of engagement are written with three major considerations in mind:

1. *Rules of employment of the force* These rules are instructions defined at the politico-military level. They are applicable to all forces committed to the theatre. These rules define the future political end-state as well as the employment of force in time and space. They suggest constraints and define the margin for initiative which the military leaders in-theatre possess.

2. *Rules or codes of behaviour* These rules set the attitude towards populations within the framework of civil–military operations; belligerents or perpetrators of violence (with regard to deployments and movements and the will to conciliate or deter); units of the coalition; and international organizations, non-governmental organizations and the media. Under certain circumstances, these rules may be set at national or international level. These are the most difficult considerations. They constitute the very substance of 'military ethics'.

Figure 7.3: Maslow's hierarchy of needs

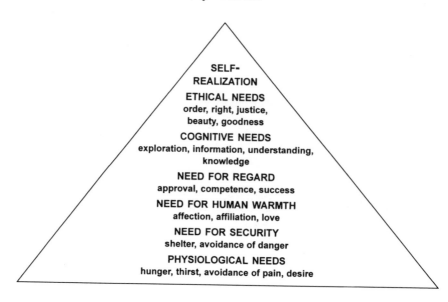

3. *Rules for the employment of weapons* These rules must include information on when to carry a gun, when to load it, when to open fire and when to return fire, and on policies on collateral damage. All this information is necessary in order to avoid the escalation of violence.

The question of morale raises the issue of the relationship between the professional requirements of military life and the social aspirations of civil life in both peacetime and wartime. One of the first purposes of social and political organizations is the satisfaction of the needs of each citizen. Abraham H. Maslow has shown the diversity of human aspirations through the 'hierarchy' or 'pyramid' of needs (Figure 7.3). To fulfil physical needs, affective (emotional) needs, intellectual needs and lastly spiritual needs, is the aspiration of civil society. As a citizen, the soldier has a legitimate right to satisfy these needs.

At the same time, however, and in order to conduct his mission successfully, the soldier must be permanently ready to face adverse circumstances. The operational context raises situations in which physical needs

Figure 7.4: Needs vs the reality of war

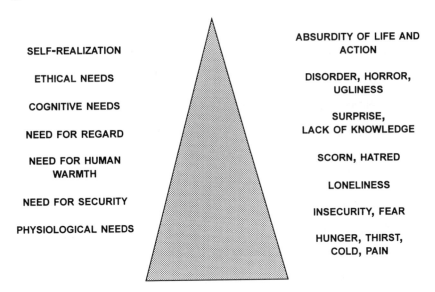

SELF-REALIZATION	ABSURDITY OF LIFE AND ACTION
ETHICAL NEEDS	DISORDER, HORROR, UGLINESS
COGNITIVE NEEDS	SURPRISE, LACK OF KNOWLEDGE
NEED FOR REGARD	
NEED FOR HUMAN WARMTH	SCORN, HATRED
	LONELINESS
NEED FOR SECURITY	INSECURITY, FEAR
PHYSIOLOGICAL NEEDS	HUNGER, THIRST, COLD, PAIN

are not satisfied, affective needs are denied and spiritual needs are set against the permanent nonsense of war. All the requirements of supporting the morale of troops depend on the capability to reconcile the often conflicting relationship between the needs of the soldier and the reality of war as represented by Figure 7.4.

Lessons learned over the last decade have shown that the qualities of being a 'good soldier' often require a reversal of Maslow's hierarchy of needs (see Figure 7.5). This requires self-discipline of a high order. To a certain degree, the soldier's desire to fulfil the mission becomes stronger than the urge to meet his primary needs. Closer analysis shows that in fact the ranking is not consistent. The distinction must be made between 'satisfiers' and 'dissatisfiers' (technical terms used by Maslow and other behavioural scientists). Shelter, food, security are needs in a sense because if they are not provided owing to operational circumstances, they will have an effect on morale. But even if these needs are provided, they do not necessarily have a positive influence on morale – only a negative influence if they are not satisfied. A strong interest in the mission has a profound and positive influence on the motivation of personnel.

Figure 7.5: Inversion of needs for being a good soldier

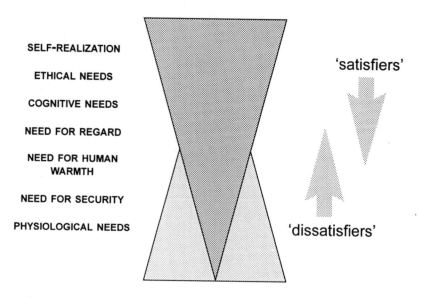

SELF-REALIZATION

ETHICAL NEEDS

COGNITIVE NEEDS

NEED FOR REGARD

NEED FOR HUMAN
WARMTH

NEED FOR SECURITY

PHYSIOLOGICAL NEEDS

'satisfiers'

'dissatisfiers'

Let me address briefly the concepts of *esprit de corps* and cohesion. *Esprit de corps* cultivates the individual's pride in being part of a group. There is a personal need for recognition in the collective identity (for example, the regiment). *Esprit de corps* can be reinforced by several factors:

- Effective intervention linked with the pride to serve
- Interest in the mission among the forces involved
- Relations with population
- The feeling of being helpful and useful
- Comparison with other units (for example, comparisons of discipline and behaviour)
- Provision of the necessities of life – supplies, security, health and comfort.

Cohesion is not a foundation or a condition of morale but the result of human relations within a limited group. It constitutes a stronghold of morale. Cohesion is the element which keeps a group together in a hostile, uncertain and chaotic environment. It is based on two basic needs identified by Maslow: a need for camaraderie, good understanding, single-mindedness in adverse situations, and a need for personal recognition by the rest of the group. Recognition stems from the fact that everyone has a role to play if the group, the squad or the section is to be efficient. Proper cohesion and *esprit de corps* make it possible to overcome problems caused by the clash of personal needs and reality with the operational environment.

To conclude, I propose that morale and motivation are two parts of an indivisible whole. Morale needs to be created. Its efficiency depends on its existence at each level. The lack of purpose at the political level or the misperception or misunderstanding of that sense makes it difficult to establish clear rules of engagement. This was exactly the case in Bosnia when our soldiers were used as hostages. Any conceptual gap is perceptible, even by a private soldier on the ground. If the overriding need to complete the mission is not supported, the failure to achieve this contributes to a decline in his morale. However, the fulfilment of these needs would have only a neutral effect. *Esprit de corps* and the ability of the group to create cohesion in the face of adversity are what is essential.

8 Building the moral component

Patrick Mileham

The one-time simplicities of moral judgment that military commanders expected to face have been replaced by the huge and persistent complexities of modern-day operations. International law, the legality of operations and the ways and means of using military force have been discussed in principle and analysed in actual operational contexts. Similarly the concerns of multinational force commanders for the morale and motivation of military units and individuals have been brought to our attention. I shall bring this volume full circle, to where military ethics should first be studied and fostered – in the officer academies of those countries subscribing to liberal democracy and international governance.

My first theme is that we have to consider the moral dilemmas surrounding the assumption that soldiers can be civilizers. In the past, the passing on from one generation of officers to another of the 'core-values' of correct conduct in war and other operations has been a subliminal activity, part of the received wisdom and corporate memory of a unit or, more generally, the officer corps. This has been the 'British way'. To quote from the past, 'a good chap knows what a good chap has to do and doesn't need to be told'. The danger nowadays is that in using all physical means at his disposal, allied to the conceptual thinking required to achieve the military task, the commander may yet discover that circumstances render him morally impotent. To get things right morally, he needs all the psycho-philosophical wisdom of a superman.

Seriously difficult problems are encountered by modern-day armed forces performing extraordinarily sophisticated military roles and tasks. All service personnel have to cope with an endless number of moral variables, internal contradictions and paradoxes. The tasks are often not merely military tasks; they are political, legal, psycho-social, economic, medical, humanitarian and, above all, dynamic practical complexities as well. When to use force or when not to use force, and why, pose intellectual and moral dilemmas which may of an instant face any military person. The need to act swiftly when presented with an instant problem may not allow sufficient time to apply any depth of intellectual and moral reasoning.

The British army's ethos statement promotes 'that spirit which inspires soldiers to fight. It derives from, and depends upon, the high degrees of commitment, self-sacrifice and mutual trust which are together so essential to the maintenance of morale.' It presupposes clear answers to the meaning of 'to fight', which may or may not mean to kill, injure and destroy, to threaten, coerce or employ other disarming tactics. What constitutes the spirit to keep the peace? Commitment, self-sacrifice and mutual trust are variables, dependent on and reciprocal with other, external variables. In terms of straightforward military discipline and the achievement of the mission, the distinction between a hypothetical and a categorical military imperative which has to be obeyed can become blurred, even in a supreme moment of consciousness. In the incident in Northern Ireland when Corporal Clegg's fourth bullet was deemed by the civil court to be the murderous one, the first, second and third ones were not. When does acting in good faith become acting in bad faith? One does not normally expect to educate soldiers in psycho-philosophy. They are trained chiefly to interpret their rules of engagement, which are carried around on a small card – supposedly condensed from thick law books – giving guidance on the practical application of the law. The spirit behind and beyond and above the law usually remains unarticulated.

The point is that in military activities, the serviceman or woman needs to be predisposed towards acting swiftly and correctly, when correctly may have wide-ranging physical, intellectual and moral ramifications. We have to assume the 'strategic corporal' will get it right. The philosopher Alasdair MacIntyre has stated that moral agents are held 'responsible' in three ways – for their 'actions which are intentional', 'for the incidental aspects of those actions of which they should have been aware' and 'for some of the reasonably predictable effects of their actions'. We have heard of the dilemmas in Kosovo in these respects, both on the ground and in the air. Intuition, the instantaneous faculty including cognitive inference, as distinct from reactive instinct, is a human capability that arguably can be educated and developed. But getting it morally wrong can endanger your life, liberty and career, as well as the life, liberty and career of others. The whole mission's moral justification can be destroyed too, as our previous speakers have shown with examples from recent events.

Young officers, in particular, need to recognize that their business is like that of surgeons and their teams. The term 'non-maleficence' can be ascribed to both the medical and the military professions. The soldier, sailor or airman legitimately kills, wounds, destroys, coerces or threatens when his orders to achieve a military objective are clear. The action should be conducted in an objective, non-maleficent spirit, even when under severe psychological pressure and actual danger. The paradox is that what he is doing under one set of temporarily suspended rules is unlawful and bad, but when he is authorized, he has to assume he is performing the same acts for the greater good of local and global humanity, as part of a grander scheme of things. He has to believe that the only legitimate object of military operations is the promise of a better peace. All of this underlies the concept of the 'civilized soldier', an oxymoron of considerable complexity. A new ethos statement may be written for operations other than war – 'that spirit which inspires a soldier to civilize others'.

My second theme has to do with conscious choice. There seems to be a general assumption that members of the armed forces in a modern liberal democracy should be all-volunteer. The ancient Greeks attributed military service to full citizenship. We do not, although there lingers a feeling in some countries that conscription is justified as 'national service' and citizenship training. Moral behaviour, however, implies choice, and as the ethicist Lady Warnock has reminded us, 'all moral choices must be free' by definition. Understanding how wide or restricted is the serviceman's freedom to choose informs the whole purpose of this book. How disciplined, then, is the training of our servicemen and women to be, and how liberal the education of our officers?

Voluntarism as the basis of our armed services implies choice in three military contexts: the willingness to join the armed services in the first place; the continuing desire to remain in service; and the most variable of the three, the willingness to fight, to impose peace or do anything else required of military servants of the state. Aristotle defines choice as that which 'may be deemed either thought related to desire or desire related to thought; and man, as an originator of action, is a union of desire and intellect'. If 'desire' is the expression of the collective mission, then the individuals who have chosen to be members of the armed forces and are in the theatre of operations more or less willingly should engage their emotions closely with the mission, and they should do so both as individuals and collectively, even if intellectually they are bound to think with military objectivity. Traditional training for fighting wars assumes that in order to achieve overwhelming force, emotions have to be blunted, if only to protect participants from psychological damage. That is the reason for a disciplinary regime for total war. Cynicism and callousness, however, have no place in what we consider to be the main purposes of modern-day expeditionary operations.

Self-discipline is the mark of moral maturity, and is highly desirable, as General Sir Rupert Smith has stated. The concept contains elements of choice, however. Is the process of maturation to be speeded up by militaristic discipline in training and subsequent service for all officers and soldiers, the vast majority of whom are in their teens or early twenties? Nowadays liberal democracies seem to impose on their armed forces a softening of discipline. The shock of military operations and the atrocities witnessed by our arguably more sensitive soldiery, including a higher proportion of women soldiers, cause psychiatric problems which have to be treated medically, not ignored, as hitherto they tended to be.

Much of the time, discipline and self-discipline are habits of mind, thus by definition subconscious. We should define ethics, or moral philosophy, as a matter of the intellect, while categorically morality and morals are about action and behaviour. Moral action implies choice and choice implies consciousness – awareness of self and circumstances. To act morally, one infers that the serviceman needs to be 'directly and authentically seized of the present state and workings of his own mind', in the words of the psycho-philosopher Gilbert Ryle. Our mental state is infinitely variable, with an inner world of its own, but it is able to grasp external circumstances and events. Full consciousness is generally described as our acute state of awareness – of ourselves and our own actions in direct relationship with our surroundings and the actions of others – in real time. Yet we cannot be fully conscious all the time. 'Imagine', stated the neuroscientist Susan Greenfield in this context, 'living in a world where everything has significance.' So consciousness is not the normal state, hour by hour, day by day, of most people. We are creatures of habit, of habitual thought and habitual actions – on 'autopilot', if one needs a simple analogy.

Yet there are moments when the soldier, sailor or airman needs to be fully conscious, in a practical, intellectual and now moral sense, at moments of choice. Supreme 'moments of truth' may be rare in their career – less rare, one assumes, for officers and certainly less rare for those on operations, when they may be sudden and cataclysmic.

How does one train or educate people to be fully morally conscious? As has been described by the neurologist John McCrone, 'consciousness is the arrival at a mental point from which everything that has happened so far falls into sharper, more coherent perspective'. Moral choices at the 'moment of truth' may not be obvious, may not be imaginable in advance. But for the officer or serviceman everything that goes before in his life, his nature, education, training, experience and capacity both for imagination and moral judgment, predisposes him to cope with an event and an action. His action may join in with a myriad of other people's 'moments of truth', and their combined actions may help to win the war or promote the peace – or fail in the attempt.

Occasionally, as we have discussed, one individual, maybe the force commander himself or maybe a private soldier or lone pilot, performs the one significant action which brings success to the whole mission – or failure. In the subsequent 'lessons learnt' exercise, that one significant action may be recognized and chronicled; or, as Tolstoy suggested, it may have been lost among the millions of unrecorded actions of ordinary people. There should be a moral to every military story, and it is the responsibility of officers, whatever their rank, to find the moral and draw others' attention to it. Debriefing should not be a pedantic afterthought, and CNN are interested anyway, as are the enemy and armchair strategists.

But moral choice is not just a matter for commanders and officers. Somehow, we must educate all service personnel to be morally conscious because, whether they like it or not, they are likely to be held morally responsible for their actions.

My third point is that before we can effectively educate people, we need to be clear about definitions – in this context particularly the terms 'integrity', 'trust' and 'morale'. Like 'leadership', unfortunately they have become short-hand expressions for a great deal of very hard-to-describe moral phenomena. I shall attempt to define each in turn.

Integrity, I believe, is that faculty of our character whereby what we say is what we do; what we promise, we deliver; what we believe in, we practise openly in our lives: our private behaviour and our inner thoughts are outwardly manifest in actions of good faith. Furthermore, what we say we will not do, for good reason, we do not do. Previous generations would have understood this as the binding agreement of a gentleman. Needless to say we do not always, or indeed often, succeed in all we try to achieve. Integrity describes what should be the whole indivisible person – colloquially, one who is not 'two-faced'. Shakespeare sums up the person of integrity through the words of Polonius, using a self-conscious paradox:

> This above all: to thine own self be true,
> And it must follow, as the night the day,
> Thou canst not then be false to any man.

But this sort of 'being true' requires the 'above all' quality which, Sir Winston Churchill noted, 'guarantees all others' – courage.

You cannot order someone to have integrity, courage and moral imagination. Such intangible predispositions can only be part of self-discipline, derived from an enlightened spirit of corporate discipline. Heavy-handed discipline is counter-productive in today's volunteer armed forces. In dangerous military operations, it is usually too late.

But what does the expression to 'be true' mean? We have to sort out in our minds and the minds of those for whom we are responsible a number of very difficult moral distinctions at the domestic military unit level and at the operational level too. We have to distinguish between opposites, which may be compared with judging all the inferences and shades of meaning in between, as well as the different nuances between nouns, adjectives and adverbs. We observe what is right and wrong, true and false, good and evil, sincerity and insincerity, honesty and dishonesty or what is fair or unfair, selfish or unselfish, just or unjust, pleasing or displeasing. The opposite of right action may be action that is wrong, or inappropriate or disproportional or accidental. Making distinctions is not to be dismissed as playing with words, when lives hang on the ability to interpret circumstances with all their moral connotations as well as the very meaning of words and different languages. Still on the subject of interpretation, one hears tell in operations of the difficulty many individuals have in recognizing whether they are witnessing reality or unreality. How do we know when we are facing a *real* moment of truth?

Taking the expression 'mutual trust' from the British army's ethos statement and connecting it with 'integrity', we find that members of our armed forces are required to be well 'integrated' into effective military units, which say what they can do and do it. This is best shown in a diagram (Figure 8.1).

Figure 8.1: Integration in effective military units

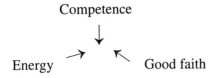

These terms signify

- the competence of individuals and units realized by possessing high degrees of knowledge, understanding and skills;
- the energy and willingness to act swiftly and for long periods, if necessary;
- good faith, the moral imperative behind all corporate and individual actions.

These components of mutual trust meet the scrutiny of psychologists as well as of philosophers, and they can be commended for any organization, whether military, other public-sector, commercial or private.

In human terms, people of high professional integrity should join together to form a spirit of corporate integrity of their group, whether section, crew, unit, field force or joint-service and multinational strategic force. That is the living 'ethos' of the force. We imply too the unity of command, of direction as well as physical, conceptual and moral cohesiveness. The opposite is unit or force disintegration, which can be the result of physical, conceptual or moral mismanagement, just as much as external forces and ill-fortune. The strength of corporate integrity is part of a unit and force morale. A military unit or force can be demoralized to extinction too.

I have heard and agree with what General Smith and Brigadier Francart have said about morale. *Esprit de corps*, regimental ethos, a general spirit of corporate optimism may appear to suggest that morale is a predisposition whole and complete of itself. In trying to understand it, we have to admit that it is not a single predisposition, existing or developed within a person or group. It is the consequential spirit or ethos, naturally synthesized from many other dynamic and circumstantial factors and events. Morale can be degraded quickly, even instantaneously, during military operations. It can take years to rebuild. Officer cadets, newly joined soldiers, sailors and airmen are required to prove 'commitment' – to take the word from the British army's ethos statement. Reciprocally they need to be satisfied with proof that their chosen service always acts for the best in its missions and provides the best means of support. In their turn, as officers and NCOs, they should provide the same best support for new intakes and generations. This is the 'maintenance of morale' in the long term and why it is a principle of war. I believe the consensus of opinion is that in the expeditionary era, moral conduct on operations is at once a vital constituent and a consequence of morale.

I am sure we all subscribe to the view that successful unit and force integration is achieved through the leadership skills of military commanders. Self-consciousness at the 'moment of truth', which tends to unnerve individuals and sometimes whole units, can be mitigated by work on building up corporate self-confidence and self-discipline in advance, to meet any contingency. These two military virtues are vital in order to promote and maintain morale. Among the other requirements of leaders is the ability to simplify complex problems in their own minds without being trapped in simple-minded optimism about practical or moral detail, and then capture the imagination of the led. It is also the ability to initiate and see appropriate action through to completion. Success of itself raises and maintains morale, which leads to further success. Truly successful leaders, however, know they should not be complacent about either success or morale.

Military ethics lies beyond and above the rules of engagement and the negative constraints of international law. It needs to be understood as the spirit of the law, suggesting and enabling military action. My final comments are about spreading that understanding. A quite recent and positive trend is to provide codes of conduct for armed forces, to assist in understanding the best sort of behaviour, derived from doctrine. They are very difficult to draw up for the reader and to be accepted as credible. The British army's *Values and Standards* code has taken four years to write. The Canadian Defence Forces version is reproduced with these papers (see pp. 86–7). The *Britannia Guide to Military Ethics* is unashamedly an explanation of moral philosophy. These codes are not orders and instructions. They constitute doctrine whose true value is realized when it is discussed and debated, as part of the military education of servicemen and women, of every rank, and then put into practice.

Let us not underestimate our junior ranks. They can take round-table discussion on matters of military morality with enthusiasm, as the Canadian Defence Forces do, even if they continue to look for leadership and example from their seniors. They can grasp right and wrong and all the shades in between. They can understand moral imperative, duties and obligations as well as moral restraint and scrutiny. Their moral imagination, judgment and integrity can be developed fully, so that the morale of their unit can be promoted and maintained to a high level, while they remain alert to moral as well as physical danger.

Above all, young officers need to develop a degree of moral maturity perhaps ahead of their years. Aristotle, early in the history of military philosophy, asserted 'we become good by doing good things and having the right emotions'. Counsels of perfection, I admit, but it is at officer academies such as Sandhurst that the education and development of military virtues begin. At the heart of the teaching must be the principle that moral authority is now the basis for all military action. Might is frequently wrong in today's world. Knowing when it is right is the moral challenge.

9 Syndicate A discussion

Anthony Hartle

What political circumstances justify military intervention?

Professor Adam Roberts raised questions about Paddy Ashdown's four criteria for the political circumstances that would justify military intervention. Sir Paddy had cited the following:

- All diplomatic alternatives are exhausted (last resort).
- Gross violations of international law or human rights are occurring.
- The violations of international law or human rights are causing widespread instability.
- Intervention is both militarily and politically practical.

Professor Roberts noted that such criteria, if they became doctrine, would bind NATO countries and others in ways that might be dysfunctional. As a result, flexibility in determining national policy and interests could suffer.

However, it was concluded that political leaders must discuss criteria for intervention and show that they will be, or were, met in all instances. In rallying and sustaining public and political support, political leaders cannot avoid establishing such criteria if they hope to be successful. Without discussing the reasons for intervention, and thus revealing the criteria supporting the decision, political leaders cannot be persuasive, either at home or abroad. Further, the criteria may well serve to protect sovereignty rather than endanger it if they establish limits for the use of force.

There is much similarity between the East Timor, Kosovo and Chechnya conflicts with respect to intervention. The intervention in East Timor would not have been possible without the precedent of Kosovo, but, by the same token, Russia would not have been as confident in its second assault on Chechnya without NATO's example. With respect to intervention in the latter two instances, however, the reality is that national interests dominate the political justification for military intervention.

The British prime minister Tony Blair certainly incorporated national interests in his Chicago speech of 22 April 1999, making them his fifth criterion for intervention. His reasoning was of particular interest, in that it represented an abrupt shift in the traditional view of the Balkans, claiming that the region is part of Europe. Thus, according to Mr Blair, offences against the Kosovar Albanians constituted offences against Europeans and, by inclusion, against British interests. This demanded a response.

The view that customary law has changed to an extent and now gives at least some legitimacy to humanitarian intervention also influences the evaluation of NATO's action. In a sense, ethical considerations seem to be superseding the cumbersome process of treaty law, and may be shaping the evolution of customary law.

The syndicate group largely agreed that the timing of NATO's military intervention in Kosovo was unfortunate. Some participants argued that the intervention was too late, in that earlier action could have minimized civilian suffering. Others maintained that the intervention was too early, because further diplomatic options were available, even though the Rambouillet talks, arguably, were a diplomatic disaster which had painted NATO into a corner. Another viewpoint suggested that events were set in motion in 1991, when the European Community told Milosevic to stop his assault on Dubrovnik – or else. When he did not stop, and Europe and NATO took no action, the long learning curve began that continued throughout the Bosnia conflict and ended (for the time being) in Kosovo. In this view, Rambouillet was only a step in the chain of events, not a seminal occurrence.

Overall, the syndicate's discussion concluded that political justification for military intervention must include the following:

- the state of international law, both positive and customary, concerning the use of force;
- the involvement of national interests;
- the possibility for alternative diplomatic efforts to resolve the crisis or ameliorate violations of rights;

- the degree of domestic engagement and support;
- the likelihood of success, which directly incorporates consideration of availability of assets and the cost of achieving acceptable results.

Kosovo: the ethical implications

Discussion focused on three issues, each related to the ethical legacy of the Kosovo campaign: technology, legal issues and mission command.

Technology

Kosovo reinforced the role of precision weapons established so dramatically in the Gulf War of 1990–1. The expectation that war will be waged with weapons that are highly discriminatory generated widespread disbelief that NATO could have bombed the Chinese embassy by mistake. Indeed, before long a decision not to use the weapon that causes the minimum collateral damage may be considered a crime.

Another concern that technology raises is the ease with which a state or coalition may decide to initiate warfare. If the weapons are seen to be politically 'clean' and the war can be prosecuted with negligible friendly losses, military intervention may prove deceptively attractive. As a result of Kosovo, we know that we must guard against that tendency.

It is also important to recognize the importance of establishing strategic objectives and plans for achieving those objectives, given a variety of circumstances. NATO initiated the war against Serbia without adequately considering a course of action – and its implications – that would follow if Milosevic refused to capitulate. NATO did not even clearly define the enemy. It said it was attacking the Milosevic regime, not the Serbian people, but as days became weeks it attacked targets that caused extensive suffering, both near- and long-term, to the Serbian populace. Even NATO target listing revealed the split focus: the categories of counter-force, counter-regime and counter-population were used. The legacy of the war tells us that we need to be quite clear about our objectives. We need to think through how to use force, especially our capability to hit targets precisely, so that we use it efficiently to attain military and political objectives. Much of the force exerted in the Kosovo campaign did not do so.

Even though Kosovo was an air war, its aftermath reinforces the lessons of Bosnia which clearly reveal one certainty: the status of soldiers is changing. The responsibilities placed on junior officers and sergeants are greater today than ever before, as interventions and peacekeeping operations dominate military activity. Military leaders must prepare soldiers on the ground to make decisions that can affect not only significant tactical developments but even strategic considerations. The actions of one soldier can have repercussions at the national level.

Legal issues

One result of the increasing transparency of military operations in the expeditionary era has been a continually increasing role for legal advisers. For a long period in the United States military lawyers have reviewed war plans for legal sufficiency. Yet only since the Gulf War have lawyers been deeply involved in current operations. In the British army legal advisers have played a significant role since Bloody Sunday in Northern Ireland in 1972. In Kosovo daily target lists received legal review. The legal aspect has achieved such prominence that we must consciously avoid the assumption that an operation is morally acceptable simply because it has received legal approval. Commanders should not shift ethical evaluation to the legal staff: moral judgment remains in the commander's hands.

The legal aspect has also been enhanced by the trend in the news media away from narrative to comment. News reporting now commonly evaluates, in addition to narrating events in front-page stories, without making clear the boundary between fact and opinion. An atmosphere of litigiousness envelops expeditionary operations.

Mission command

That same trend and the information age more generally have made the avoidance of casualties a dominating concern. Risk-free operations have become the standard, even to the extent of influencing the commonly understood contract between the soldier and the state. Today we find a greater expectation on the part of both the public and members of the military that a commitment of military forces abroad will include a commitment to minimize friendly casualties. A direct consequence of the Gulf War and now Kosovo is the extent to which politicians tend to mislead their constituents in the belief that we shall always be able to fight without casualties. This tendency becomes a trap in reverse, in that political leaders will be reluctant to commit forces, even in the best of causes, if the military cannot assure them that the conflict can be fought with minimum casualties.

Concerns about publicity, about casualties and about legal considerations have in turn generated great attention to the rules of engagement. The fact that different countries have considerably different rules of engagement – from the Germans, with the most restrictive rules, to the British, who have the most liberal ones – suggests that this is an area of potential concern in respect to professionally acceptable conduct. When forces from different countries with different RoE work together in expeditionary interventions, as United Nations forces in KFOR must do, a variety of issues involving ethical concerns may arise.

Coalition operations and sensitivity to public opinion have also made honesty a casualty to some extent since Kosovo, perhaps even more so than in the Gulf War. In that conflict, the tendency was to suppress bad news. In Kosovo we saw a persistent attempt to 'spin' results, both in terms of coalition politics and battlefield activity. The result was a decline in the credibility of official spokesmen and governments.

Other issues

There were two other ethical issues in the Kosovo campaign. First was the strengthening of the conditionality of the principle of sovereignty and its corollary, the principle of non-intervention. Since the end of the Kosovo campaign, the United Nations Secretary-General and others have buttressed the significance of human rights and the authority of external authorities to intervene in the domestic affairs of sovereign states when widespread and serious human rights violations occur. Certainly East Timor would not have been treated as it was if the Kosovo intervention had not occurred. If we again faced the imminent bloodbath that occurred in Rwanda in 1994, the reaction of international community today would be far different.

The second obvious and difficult lesson of Kosovo is the claim that when necessary and sufficient conditions for intervention are met, military intervention is not only permissible but also morally obligatory. Although we have no consensus on Paddy Ashdown's criteria or any other set of criteria, we do face a growing sense that the moral response has become a mandate to act. Failure to respond requires justification.

The syndicate concluded that Kosovo generated a variety of critically important ethical concerns. These must be worked through, with the development of new and coherent responses, if we are to avoid undermining respect for individuals and for international humanitarian law, the very causes for which we now so frequently take up arms and for which we put our military forces at risk.

Building force and unit morale and motivation

In the presentations and discussions concerning ethics in the expeditionary era, the syndicate recognized three distinct levels of consideration. The first level examined the convergence of global institutions and supranational authority. While global institutions are certainly in the very early stages of development, sovereign nations no longer have what once was nearly full control over domestic affairs. Agencies external to the state directly influence economic affairs, disseminate information that the state cannot censor or manage, and also impose legal requirements.

The second level encompasses domestic affairs and national decision-making. Michael Ignatieff addressed this level when he discussed the shallow public support that exists for humanitarian intervention in comparison with military operations that directly affect national interests. Unlike wars of survival or the use of force clearly necessitated by national interests, humanitarian intervention receives support only as long as the public perceives that casualties are minimal and costs reasonable.

The third level focuses on the soldier, the captain or the corporal, who is on the ground and making both routine and critical decisions which can determine the success or legitimacy of the intervention as a whole. The syndicate explored whether there were linkages between these levels that shed light on morale and motivation.

In discussing cultural differences that might complicate motivation and morale, some group members maintained that a significant gulf separates European and American attitudes towards waging war. An anecdote revealing that gulf concerns a briefing by an American general at Hurlbutt Field (an airfield in Florida) shortly before the initiation of the relief operation in Somalia. The general referred to the forces of General Mohammed Aideed as 'the enemy', even though the operation was designed, initially, as one of humanitarian relief. The American mentality, this view contends, sees conflict as a win-or-lose proposition. Europeans note that American sporting events do not end in a draw, while the most popular sport in Europe, soccer, frequently does. In that vein, the European mentality, which extends to soldiers, accepts more readily that an expeditionary operation may have as its objective the achievement or maintenance of conditions which make it possible to resolve a situation without taking actions that establish partiality between warring factions. Such cultural differences will, in fact, create different considerations with respect to morale and motivation.

Public perceptions influence political decision-makers, most obviously in democratic states. Public perceptions in turn are shaped by media reporting and commentary. Syndicate members cited instances ranging from Somalia to Kosovo in which a single picture presented by the media mobilized public opinion more effectively than any political appeal could have done. Given today's immediacy of communications, public perceptions and questions also reach deployed soldiers rapidly and forcefully, sometimes with dramatic effect on morale and motivation. The injunction to be straightforward and candid with the media creates challenging dilemmas for commanders, who recognize the impact that public perceptions can have on the effectiveness of their soldiers, especially if the force consists of a variety of national contingents. Thus the effectiveness of the captain and the corporal, who carry a great weight of responsibility, becomes a matter of not only tactical but also strategic concern. If they make the wrong decisions, they can bring about the failure of national projects.

10 Syndicate B discussion

Paul Maillet

In considering issues of ethics in intervention operations in the expeditionary era, emerging areas of concern are the justification of military intervention, the moral and legal handcuffing of the military and the need to build and maintain unit and force morale.

If these issues are combined with the various revolutions currently sweeping the armed forces and society, there is no doubt that the military will never be the same again. The *technological* revolution (which requires high levels of education and knowledge), the *social* revolution (which demands a rights-based military force that reflects societal values such as gender, diversity, respect and human rights) and the *transparency* revolution (with its all-seeing and instantaneous media involvement) are all rapidly transforming military accountability. This is complicated by the emergence of the corporal as a 'strategic corporal', whose decisions – and their consequences – are broadcast live to the world and can greatly influence policy at the strategic level.

There would appear to be an increasing link between the *jus ad bellum* (of conflict) and the *jus in bello* (in conflict) dimensions of these issues. The educated volunteer soldier of today has a critical interest, and greater stake, in strategic policy and decisions. These soldiers expect and deserve clear and honest explanations of policy to which they can commit themselves and which act as a rational basis for motivation and morale. There is an obvious social trend emerging which is redefining the social contract between soldiers, the military and governments. This leads to broader questions, such as the extent to which soldiers are merely tools of the state and the extent to which they are moral agents in their own right. We may be moving towards the realization of the Kantian imperative, which proposed that everyone is of equal moral worth and deserves to be treated in themselves as ends rather than means.

Justifying military intervention

The circumstances and criteria that justify military intervention can be very complex. One interesting approach to the question is from the point of view of ethical 'rights' versus 'duties'. Do we have a right to intervene? If so, then on what basis? Does this right confer a duty to do so? These questions have implications both for the role of the soldier and for outside perceptions of this role.

It would be useful to determine what the soldier thinks about intervention. The social contract with the soldier in many countries is understood to suggest that he or she serves to fight for the vital interests of the nation, usually with regard to issues of national survival, or to prevent harm to national citizens. As military intervention missions become predominant, the question arises whether or not the soldier signed up to risk his or her life for non-vital, ambiguous humanitarian missions in distant countries. To what extent does the soldier agree with this new role? What are the expectations that must be changed for soldiers to commit themselves to these new roles?

From an external perspective, the essential requirement is to provide 'justification' to external audiences of the need to intervene and the action itself, and to do so in a compelling manner. In ethical terms, this justification needs a supporting doctrine of rights and freedoms. Without such a doctrine, *ad hoc* arguments and arrangements could be subject to inconsistency and manipulation by belligerents and the media. But although there is a need to justify the desired action to the international community, the criteria for intervention do not necessarily need to be preset. The justification could depend on circumstances and any applicable logical model. There is no compelling need to be limited to a specific set of criteria. Arguments could be based on the preconditions discussed by Paddy Ashdown (for example, diplomatic failure, gross violation of human rights, regional stability and reasonable prospects of success). Also, there are the just war criteria (legitimate authority, just cause, last resort, proportionality). In the discussion, moral principles were articulated to suggest a reasoning process to determine if an ethical problem in fact requires action. The first principle was *need*, a compelling need in which some significant harm was possible. The second was *proximity*, in which the agent either knows of the need or can reasonably be shown to be aware of the need. The third was *capability*, in which the agent has the means to do something about the need. The fourth related to the agent as the person of *last resort*: if the agent does not help, then no one else is likely to do so.

The point is that any criteria can be acceptable if they convince the international community of the requirement for and legitimacy of action, provided that they are based on generally accepted ethical and legal principles and are validated to some extent by the formation of a 'consensus of the willing' or another global response that leads to corrective action. It may well be that the planning depth, or the 'art of the possible', of the response to a crisis is limited in order to avoid forcing decisions that conflict with national points of view and that would hinder or stall the intervention process.

Following the establishment of a right to intervene, one justified and accepted by the international community, the question arises of the duty to act. Whether or not to intervene – with attendant difficulties of cost, long-haul potential, sustainability, political issues and some sort of threshold of minimal altruism (ironically causing more harm to the intervening military agent than the good his action was intended to achieve) – is a difficult decision. Examples of intervention with extensive obligations for reconstruction, involving long-term and expensive operations, include Cyprus and Northern Ireland.

Another approach as an alternative to long-term and expensive commitment involves the theory of 'breaking the cycle of violence'. This approach advocates the creation of an enforced pause in violence. It is based on the theory that a cessation of violence will create an aversion or reluctance to return to it, particularly after the belligerents have experienced a period of relative peace and security, and this will allow the intervening forces to withdraw. An example would be the Kurdish action after the Gulf War.

In most situations, decisions to not intervene were deemed to hold significant risks. Letting issues and events run their course was fraught with risk. The horrific example of Rwanda will forever give pause to the judgment that leans towards non-intervention.

Handcuffing the military

In considering constraints on the military, there is a premise that the use of force requires limits and controls. Many questions arise from this. Who imposes the constraints? How are they dealt with? How does a military force deal ethically with the complications of transparency? Limits and controls depend largely on the extent of the trust and confidence in the military force to do the right thing in high-intensity ethical dilemmas. This depends on many factors. One factor is the moral maturity or psychology of the soldier and how individual differences in maturity are managed by the military force. Most military forces consist of soldiers of ages from 18 to 45. Most exhibit the full spectrum of moral development. The literature of psychology generally describes moral development as in three stages. The first consists of exerting influence through rewards and punishment. The second involves identification with peer groups, of particular significance in small military units and extending to social groups and expectations (for example, to obey the law). Third, the highest level of moral development is that of principled behaviour. People committed to universal principles of justice or care will stand up to adverse group or external pressures. The inevitable tension between the law, ethics and psychology creates significant challenges which, if not handled correctly, can result in criminal behaviour or post-traumatic stress disorder casualties. Feelings of helplessness, an inability to exercise the moral ethics of care and exposure to atrocities or traumatic events are serious concerns that can have significant effects on individuals involved in peacekeeping or intervention missions.

Within this tension, the decision-making environment complicates the responsibility of the soldier to be ethically correct. Decisions are influenced by the values, beliefs and individual differences of the soldiers, the moral intensity of the situation and the ethical climate of the unit or military force. The ethical climate includes the opportunity for the leadership to exert the most influence. If the ethical climate supports ethical behaviour and encourages and rewards it, then ethical behaviour is more likely.

Another factor that makes life difficult for the military is the conflict of expectations. On the one hand, high-level intentions are translated into rules of engagement or campaign objectives, which in turn become mission or technical compliance issues. On the other hand, ethical expectations increase the imperatives to minimize collateral damage and to respect human rights, diversity, gender and other factors which translate into ethical compliance issues. How are ethical decisions made when these two sets of expectations compete or conflict? How does the military face the public when things go terribly wrong and when the ethics of the situation is hotly debated, as in the bombing of the Chinese embassy during the Kosovo conflict? Can the military distinguish between an error in judgment and a deficiency in values? Does the military have the courage to treat each case differently in terms of tolerance and forgiveness or censure? How does the military deal with the public expectations it creates by using precision-guided munitions and enhanced capabilities and by encouraging a zero casualty mentality when it fears to lose perceived shallow public support for an intervention? The debate on intolerance of casualties partly attributes this attitude to a safe, low birth rate and to an affluent and secure social environment. This is compounded by the televising of the dramatic results of strikes with highly accurate precision-guided stand-off weapons. The debate on whether we are entering an era of 'post-heroic' warfare, in which casualties are acceptable only in instances of immediate self-defence and vital national interest, merits attention. What does this mean for military deployments in the future?

As a last but critical issue, military forces are handcuffed by the very visibility that the public demands of its armed forces. The public is able to question military events and issues on which in the past it had very little information. With greater public information comes greater public accountability. In many tough ethical decisions, some degree of harm usually occurs, no matter what choice is made. As a result, 'dirty hands' are inevitable. The public therefore bids military forces a hearty welcome to the world of 'due diligence', to severe 'public scrutiny', to the 'burden of proof', to the 'reasonable person' test. These are new words in the military vernacular. They come with the strong obligation for military forces to set internal ethical expectations for which they are willing to be held accountable and to create strong rights-based social climates. Tribunals, such as the Rome tribunal, will evaluate the conduct of both victor and vanquished, and neither will escape exposure of misconduct. If we believe in ethical imperatives, this cannot be perceived as a bad thing.

Morale and intervention

The issue of building morale in the context of intervention operations requires acknowledging and addressing a number of paradigm shifts that are occurring (or that must occur) if the endstate is to be a highly motivated and ethical military force. The first paradigm shift relates to a change in the social contract that is necessary between society and the military. Military forces must wholeheartedly accept the roles of humanitarian assistance and aid to the civil power in disaster or environmental crisis, in addition to their traditional roles of deterrence and fighting. They must internalize the expectations of these new roles and broaden the understanding of what it means to be in the military. The emergence of new military roles requires armed forces to redefine themselves in terms of the future and in terms of what professional and job satisfaction means – in other words, what it means to 'feel good' about being a soldier should now have an expanded dimension. The traditional warrior ethic and the comments of 'wasting their time with peacekeeping' or dissatisfaction with 'fighting for the cause of foreign cultures' must change. The soldiers who complain of not 'feeling the hero' within their families and communities as a result of humanitarian service must not be encouraged by their leadership to cling to obsolete expectations. Peacekeeping has a measure of 'hero' status in Canada and some other Western nations, but this is not necessarily so for military forces in other countries.

A second paradigm shift relates to changing the ethos and values of the traditional military culture, which sees victory as the primary measure of success. A dilemma arises when there is a competition between the values of military victory and the values linked with the political conditions for the cessation of violence. We must broaden the concept of victory to include the conditions of impasse and containment and other, non-military objectives as defined by political authorities. The years spent in Cyprus and Korea to prevent the outbreak of war, and the limited objectives of the Gulf War and the Kosovo campaign are examples of when a total military solution was not established as the objective. Military forces must realize that they are no longer the complete solution in themselves – they are very much subordinate to the larger political solution.

A third paradigm shift pertains to collective effect. Military cultures and countries too experience difficulties in changing from what was once a strong and autonomous national all-arms, all-capability military force to one of niche strengths, reduced capabilities and increased liabilities. The issues of sharing – pooling not only precious capabilities and resources but also political risk – are not easy to resolve cleanly. The dilemma of dealing with the competing values of vital interests and 'warrior ethics' versus global moral and social rights-based ethics can create serious morale problems for a military culture entrenched in centuries of hard-won tradition. The question of which becomes the 'first order' ethic, in what circumstances, must be answered by a clear, compelling and rational justification in order for military cultures to surrender or change those beliefs and predispositions for autonomy that they have held dear.

Closing comment

The realization that ethics and moral values are playing a greater part in what was largely the realm of legal, military or political imperatives is important. The decision-making process in *jus ad bellum* (ethics of conflict) issues at the strategic level are facing new challenges such as intervention and humanitarian values and concerns. Similarly, the emerging importance of the 'strategic corporal' requires a heightened decision-making capability for *jus in bello* (ethics in operations) situations at the tactical level. The expectation is for an increased emphasis on ethics at both levels. We must ask ourselves if the corporal, the general officer and the politician all possess a consistent set of values, as well as the moral reasoning skills necessary to make the decisions that will meet both the morally heightened expectations of the public and the unrelenting scrutiny of the media. What guidance can we provide for the strategic soldier to do the right thing in high-intensity moral situations? What are the expectations we have of this soldier? In the final analysis, we must pay strict attention to the ethical dimension of decisions made at both the strategic political and tactical operational levels. They will affect our future profoundly.

Box 10.1 (a) Canadian defence ethics card

CANADIAN DEFENCE ETHICS

Principles

- Respect the dignity of all persons
- SERVE CANADA BEFORE SELF
- OBEY AND SUPPORT LAWFUL AUTHORITY

Obligations

- INTEGRITY: We give precedence to ethical principles and obligations in our decisions and actions. We respect all ethical obligations deriving from applicable laws and regulations. We do not condone unethical conduct.

- LOYALTY: We fulfil our commitments in a manner that best serves Canada, DND and the CF.

- COURAGE: We face challenges, whether physical or moral, with determination and strength of character.

- HONESTY: We are truthful in our decisions and actions. We use resources appropriately and in the best interests of the Defence mission.

- FAIRNESS: We are just and equitable in our decisions and actions.

- RESPONSIBILITY: We perform our tasks with competence, diligence and dedication. We are accountable for and accept the consequences of our decisions and actions. We place the welfare of others ahead of our personal interests.

The text of the laminated card issued to every member of the Canadian Defence Forces is presented here (Box 10.1 (a) and (b)). It shows how Canada tries to put defence ethics into practice.

Box 10.1 (b) Canadian defence ethics card (reverse)

WHAT IS AN ETHICAL DILEMMA?

- Ethics is about right and wrong
- A dilemma is a situation in which:

  You are unsure of the right thing to do.
  Two or more of our values may be in conflict:
  ie, honesty vs loyalty
  Harm may be caused, no matter what you do.

HOW DO YOU DECIDE WHAT TO DO?

- You consider your obligation to act.
- You consider the options you have.
- You choose the best option that considers:
  RULES   CONSEQUENCES
  CARE FOR OTHERS   VALUES
- If unsure, you talk to others, to those you trust, to your friends, or your superiors or authorities. Someone is prepared to listen and help, anytime you have a concern or problem.
- You accept responsibility for your actions.

HOW CAN WE ALL IMPROVE ETHICAL BEHAVIOUR?

- Leaders make the expectations, the risks, and what to do about them, very clear.
- Leaders provide opportunities to discuss concerns, or ask questions.
- Leaders take prompt action when problems occur. They ensure confidentiality and a reprisal free environment.
- We can recognise manifestly unlawful or inappropriate orders, and know that we are not required to obey them, and we will speak out.
- Whether we are a witness or someone being victimised, when unethical behaviour occurs, we have a responsibility to speak out or act.

11 Syndicate C discussion

Marisa Rodríguez Mojón

The group began its discussion by considering that the increased visibility of warfare brings increasing public scrutiny and by questioning whether this visibility is constraining. The various viewpoints expressed within the group are summarized as follows.

First, public opinion can have an important effect on military operations. Public opinion differs in different countries. It was noted that in the Netherlands, for example, the public as a whole largely backs peace-support operations – but only if they are located close to home. The sight of suffering is very much a mobilizing factor in respect to Dutch public opinion. This explains Dutch support for action in the Former Republic of Yugoslavia. Yet this factor is not always sufficient to generate support for policies of conflict prevention.

Second, the media play a very important role in the issue of ethics in modern warfare. Media access gives home populations the opportunity to scrutinize events – often very selectively. The media cover those events related to their own interests and purposes. This can bring distortion of both information and priorities. As seen in Kosovo, prospective opponents of NATO can manipulate media agendas to significant effect.

Third, the issues of intolerance for sustaining casualties and collateral damage have a significant impact on public opinion. Public opinion is influenced very strongly by issues of protecting human rights. Home populations generally are very concerned about whether what is being achieved is worth the casualties. This factor is a prominent influence in US public opinion in particular. In the Kosovo conflict, government perceptions of possible public outcry over casualties and collateral damage caused NATO's strategy to be designed specifically to minimize civilian casualties. Yet there were many instances when the implementation of the strategy failed to achieve this aim.

Fourth, and directly linked to the previous point, is the fact that it is important for governments to explain clearly the reasons for and aims of intervention – both to their public and to their soldiers – and to be able to justify these in relation to possible casualty levels. Governments should develop means for conveying this kind of information to the public instead of leaving the responsibility for this to the media.

However important the minimizing of casualties becomes as an issue, force protection – keeping soldiers out of the conflict in order to reduce risks of casualties – cannot become the main mission priority if, as a result, a mission's aims become unattainable. The mission has to be worth dying for. National leadership should be able to explain the importance of the mission to the media, to the public and to its soldiers.

The second major focus of the group's discussion was the concept of 'just war', as manifested in the terms *jus in bello* and *jus ad bellum*. Intervention in Kosovo was justified by Western governments as a response to Serbian violations of international law. NATO intervened in response to a humanitarian crisis.

Geopolitics is an important influence on the practical application of the 'just war' concept, as geostrategic purposes may conflict with meeting the challenges of high moral values. For example, in Kosovo the humanitarian crisis saw a flood of refugees heading for neighbouring countries which were not prepared – either in principle (in terms of accepting them) or in practice (in terms of having the necessary facilities) – to accommodate them. A similar refugee problem confronted the United States in Haiti in the early 1990s. Practical geostrategic constraints such as logistics also complicate moves to protect human rights, whether at a distance (as in the case of Haiti) or nearer to home (as in the case of Kosovo).

If the weight of public opinion in favour of intervention to protect human rights becomes irresistible, politicians may feel forced to intervene. In such a situation, meeting other criteria for intervention may become less important. However, it should be noted that home populations may be under the misperception that militaries have the capacity to make surgical interventions as a matter of course. The public may well change its support for certain actions if and when it realizes that this is not so.

Another crucial aspect to take into account is the fact that there is no international law which defines how a peace-support operation should be carried out. As a matter of fact, the enforcing power in Kosovo (KFOR) had to impose its law after the war had finished. Directly linked to this legal issue is the matter of the role of lawyers as advisers to the military. This is an increasing practice today. Although acting only as advisers, lawyers have a fundamental influence within the decision-making process.

The final key issue discussed by the group was the role played by soldiers in peace-support operations. This role is very different from the roles undertaken by soldiers in other kinds of war at other times in history. Effective and legitimate peace-support action requires the support not only of domestic public opinion, but also of the inhabitants of the region in question. This is why decisions and actions at the level of the 'strategic corporal' become very important. The role of the 'strategic corporal' is a day-to-day one. Corporals may find themselves placed in highly demanding situations, situations which are often redefined minute-by-minute. The soldiers must distribute food and medical supplies (for example) while continuing to keep combatants apart and defending civilians.

In view of their demanding role, corporals require special training, including clearly communicated rules of engagement (RoE). RoE help to control both the threat of crisis escalation and the possible responses to it. A question raised in discussion was whether it would be possible to develop a version of RoE specific to Europe. There was consensus within the group that this probably would be very difficult, as each country has different policies, priorities, interpretations and means for responding to the same situation.

RoE, of course, do not refer specifically to behaviour; neither can they substitute for education in ethics. Here, however, the Canadian Defence Forces, for example, have made significant achievements. Among other things, Canadian soldiers are issued with a very simple pocket card[3] – the 'Soldier's Ethics Card' – listing some basic rules concerning defence ethics and providing advice as to how to solve ethical dilemmas.

[3] See Syndicate B discussion, pp. 86–7.

12 Syndicate D discussion

Paul Cornish

In considering Adam Roberts' plenary paper on 'The Changing Form and Functions of the Laws of War', the discussion at first took a practical, 'bottom-up' approach. While the laws of war are appropriately a subject for abstract conceptualization and theorization, what also matters is how the laws are applied on the ground, and with what effect. Most military people would be familiar with the claim that the purpose of the laws of war and humanitarian arms control is to impose standards of decent behaviour to be observed during conflict. But is the normative, humanitarian project running ahead of itself, perhaps even to the extent that it has begun to crowd out military activity – as understood and experienced historically – with its propensity, and at times need, to be nasty and brutish? It may be one thing to expect to constrain the activity of warfare by humanitarian principles and rules but quite another to suppose that war itself can be made to conform to them.

Participants reflected upon the now commonplace observation that recent and projected developments in military technology (both weapon and non-weapon) seem in important respects to challenge the coherence and the distinctness of the laws of war tradition. In one much-discussed scenario a powerful missile is launched against a target from beyond visual and radar range. There is the expectation, but no guarantee, of a highly accurate strike and minimal 'collateral' damage and the near certainty that the pilot of the launching aircraft or the crew of the cruise-missile warship will be invulnerable to any response. But what does this scenario imply for the principle of discrimination, one of the two foundations of the laws of war (the second being proportionality)? Previously, combatants themselves have been expected to discriminate between military and non-military targets in their use of weaponry. Is the requirement for discrimination now to be met by technology rather than individual judgment? If so, what happens when the attack fails to be discriminate? Is this a case of personal moral and legal culpability or merely technical failure? Furthermore, does the expectation (or perhaps fact) of impunity on the part of the attacker alter the fundamental nature of the activity, war, which the various rules and guidelines have for centuries sought to constrain? The laws of war have developed to address impartially the activity of warfare as a whole rather than the behaviour of one side or the other, aggressor or defender, in a conflict. The object of these laws has been to moderate the infliction and receipt of violence and barbarity by both sides, each of which was therefore assumed to have a stake in the implementation and observance of the various codes of conduct. It is an entirely different proposition which says that the laws of war are to protect the militarily weak against the stronger, invulnerable side. The latter may have at best only a vestigial commitment to ideas and policies which seek to moderate behaviour impartially and mutually, through what might be termed enlightened self-policing. And if the laws of war are to be about protection of the vulnerable, who or what is to police and enforce those laws?

As for the intellectual, legal and practical distinctness of the laws of war (distinct, that is, from laws and principles governing recourse to armed conflict), the syndicate considered another scenario: on a politically sensitive peacekeeping operation, the gunner in a main battle tank has acquired a enemy tank target and is in a position to engage and destroy it in accordance with the rules of engagement as promulgated and understood at the tactical level. The gunner's sighting and fire control system are, however, all electronic and are being automatically relayed to a distant headquarters, where very senior military and political leaders are observing the engagement and have the communications capability to issue direct orders to the gunner. How might this level of warfare best be described: tactical, operational, military-strategic or politico-military? Do the laws of war operate in this case, or the laws of politics? Who is to blame if the 'enemy tank' is fired upon but turns out to be a pneumatic decoy positioned in front of a school?

New weapons, advanced military communications and the rapid expansion of media and civil communications all point to the need for more reflection on the question of personal responsibility. What are the limits upon and possibilities for personal judgment? Where does blame lie when mistakes are made? Are mistakes more likely as the levels of warfare and the 'levels' of ethics (*jus ad bellum* and *jus in bello*) all collapse into an all-informed but risk- and blame-averse culture? If ethics is the engagement between morality and reality, and is about choosing between competing moral imperatives, the ostensible blooming of military ethics in the past decade appears to lead in precisely the opposite direction – towards indecisiveness and moral timidity.

The discussants saw a clear need to correct this perceived imbalance, and there was broad support during discussion for the argument that the ethical and legal debate had become too fixated upon particular weapons and technologies. To restore a sense of personal responsibility, and to make coherent military activity once again a possibility, a shift towards a more consequentialist moral reasoning might be appropriate. This would allow the unpleasantness of the exercise of military force to be set against the anticipated overall good effect, and even allow for admitting the possibility that mistakes can be made in the military sphere, as in all other areas of human activity. But of course just war theory, the paradigm within which, implicitly or explicitly, much discussion took place, has a pronounced deontological character. This sense of duty associated with just war is manifested not least in the long tradition of isolating certain weapons as repugnant and banning their use on no grounds other than humanitarian obligation. And consequentialism might lure the unsuspecting towards one of the more celebrated travesties of the Vietnam war, in which a village was reputedly destroyed in order that it might be 'saved'.

In the end, the discussion of the laws of war was inconclusive. The practical, 'bottom-up' discussion led to recognition that the laws of war debate is complex and continues to be in a state of flux. But this is to be expected; after all, the laws of war are but manifestations of a complex, long-running and fluid moral project. In this context, the most that should be expected as new weapons and capabilities are developed is debate and discussion, and the up-to-date education of armed forces in the ethical dimensions of their profession. In other words, the form of the laws of war will, as in the past, require constant revision and updating, and it should be possible to make timely and valuable contributions to that process. But more interesting things could be said about the function of the laws of war. The laws of war have developed as an ethical mechanism, with their function to allow an engagement between morality and military activity. Now, however, it seems that developments in weaponry and communications may have transformed the 'moral project' into a 'moralizing project', in which morality dominates (and perhaps crowds out) rather than merely engages with military activity. Thus, while the current debate may appear to continue the long-running ethical project, wherein the laws of war are reformed to reflect new circumstances while their function remains broadly unchanged, behind the scenes the functional dimension too may be changing and expanding fundamentally. The function of the laws of war may no longer be to seek a balance between morality and military activity but to allow the overwhelming of the latter by the former. Whether deliberate or unintended, this shift would plainly represent an important change in military ethics.

Discussion turned to the ethical issues raised by NATO's operations in 1999 in and on behalf of Kosovo. Was the intervention ethical, in the sense of *jus ad bellum*? Was there a just cause? Was there a reasonable prospect of success? Had all other, non-military options been exhausted or were the Rambouillet talks a cynical attempt to goad Milosevic into providing NATO with a pretext to begin operations? There were no easy answers to these and other questions, but there was a sense that while the legality of NATO's action may be debatable, the alliance has nevertheless been left with something like a moral obligation to intervene again in the future, should similar circumstances present themselves.

Kosovo also prompted discussion of the form of military intervention. Should air power have been used massively and overwhelmingly from the outset or was it better to escalate gradually, seeking a compromise between military action and diplomatic signalling? Some might argue that the military principle of minimum effective force has now become a political tool which emphasizes 'minimum' at the expense of 'effective', thus constraining the military in the name of 'proportionality'. Is this requirement for 'proportionate' (that is, cautious and incremental) military action well-reasoned or does it reflect political and moral indecisiveness and prevarication? If the latter, does this place the safety of a state's armed forces below the interests of its political leadership, and even below the interests of the military opponent? Are we witnessing the progressive marginalization of military expertise in the politico-military decision-making process? Do political leaders generally know enough about the military profession and the exacting nature of active duty for them to make sound ethical judgments on their own terms?

The final discussion session attempted to bring the various strands of the conference together. What does this highly developed ethical debate mean, in practical terms, for armed forces? More specifically, the discussion asked, how can 'force and unit morale and motivation' be built and maintained in the context of ever more intrusive political, legal and ethical oversight of military activity? In the era of combined and multinational operations, can alliances and coalitions be expected to conform in their behaviour to a common (and expanding) ethical code? Better military education and training offer some hope of achieving a healthy relationship between the world of ethics and the military profession. Members of armed forces must be aware that they operate in a highly developed (and highly contestable) ethical climate, and they need to ensure that their thinking and judgment are mature and sophisticated. But healthy relationships are not usually achieved unilaterally; those who observe and comment upon military activity from a political, legal or moral standpoint must also be expected to evince some understanding of the special physical and moral circumstances in which the military professional operates. Critics who find themselves unable or unwilling to make such a concession run the risk of undermining the ethical project: a process intended to permit an engagement between morality and military activity may be revealed to be little more than a means to allow the moral to dominate the behavioural. This outcome would be more akin to moral absolutism than ethical evaluation.

There is a risk of expecting too little of the military, of undermining the ethical relationship by allowing the reality and exigencies of military activity to be crowded out by an unstructured, undiscriminating and overwhelming mixture of political caution and moralizing sentiment. But the ethical relationship can be corrupted in another way. There is also a risk of expecting too much of the military, of assuming that the relationship between the military and the moral can be maintained by the armed forces alone. In the British and other armed forces, the ideal of the 'strategic corporal' is well established. It refers to the military and political value of well-trained, intelligent and disciplined junior leaders, who have the confidence and professional ability to make the right decision *in extremis*. There is a sense, however, in which in the current climate 'mere' professional expertise and judgment are no longer adequate; the 'strategic corporal' must also be politically adept, legally aware and philosophically sound.

This tendency is illustrative of a relationship based not on mutual under-standing between society and political leaders, on the one hand, and the military, on the other, but on a wish to establish scapegoats and ensure that blame can be attributed when, say, a peacekeeping operation does not develop as initially expected. In this respect, the refusal of the United States to embrace the International Criminal Court may reflect reason-able reluctance to expose junior members of its armed forces to political, legal and moral jeopardy on an international scale.

Much is expected of armed forces, not least to be able to live and function in often squalid circumstances while carrying out extreme acts on behalf of society, usually at immense personal risk, and calling upon uncommon reserves of personal virtue and courage. In return, armed forces might fairly expect society and government to provide what is necessary and reasonable for their physical self-protection and would welcome caution among decision-makers and public opinion whenever military lives are at stake. But too much sensitivity – the so-called 'body-bag syndrome' – could be just as unwelcome as too little. Armed forces might also expect to be 'protected' morally from being placed in or near a conflict or crisis while being denied the means and opportunity to respond to a seen egregious abuse. And finally, armed forces might expect to share responsibility with those on whose behalf they are called upon to act and, in that respect, to be 'protected' from undue, unfair and precipitate criticism and blame.

The 'bottom-up' approach to the discussion of the place of ethics in the expeditionary era led to the conclusion that various relationships are at play: between morality and reality; between the individual and the collec-tive; between theory and practice; and, finally, between governments, the media and public opinion, on the one hand, and the armed forces, on the other. Ethics is, above all, relational. A government may instruct its armed forces to deploy here or there, to use this or that equipment or to spend only so much from the public purse. But when government and society instruct or expect armed forces to 'be more ethical', two things should be borne in mind. The first is that there could be practical impli-cations to this injunction which are either unforeseen or ill-advised from a professional military standpoint. And the second is that, unlike those activities which fall more or less exclusively within the sphere of competence of the military (that is, training men and women to be able to mount a certain type of operation when called upon to do so), 'being ethical' is not something which the military can achieve unilaterally. The many 'ethical challenges' discussed during the conference confront not only armed forces seeking to redefine themselves in the post-Cold War, expeditionary era but also the government minister, the lawyer, the ethicist, the journalist and the member of the public, all of whom should share the rewards of success, however measured, and the responsibility for failure.

Further reading

Amstutz, Mark R. (1999). *International Ethics: Concepts, Theories and Cases in Global Politics* (Lanham, MD: Rowman and Littlefield).

Annan, Kofi (1999). 'Intervention', *The Ditchley Foundation Lecture*, No. 35 (Oxford: The Ditchley Foundation).

Bellamy, Christopher (1997). *Knights in White Armour: The New Art of War and Peace* (updated edn) (London: Random House/Pimlico).

Best, Geoffrey (1980). *Humanity in Warfare: The Modern History of the International Law of Armed Conflicts* (London: Methuen).

Dallaire, General Romeo (1998). 'The End of Innocence: Rwanda 1994', in Jonathan Moore (ed.), *Hard Choices: Moral Dilemmas in Humanitarian Intervention* (Lanham, MD: Rowman and Littlefield).

Dunlap, Col. Charles J. (1991). *Technology and the 21st Century Battlefield: Recomplicating Moral Life for the Statesman and the Soldier* (Carlisle, PA: Strategic Studies Institute, US Army War College).

Glover, Jonathan (1999). *Humanity: A Moral History of the Twentieth Century* (London: Jonathan Cape).

Hables Gray, Chris (1997). *Post-modern War: The New Politics of Conflict* (London: Routledge/New York: Guildford Press).

Ignatieff, Michael (1998). *The Warrior's Honor: Ethnic War and the Modern Conscience* (London: Chatto and Windus).

Matthews, Lloyd J. and Brown, Dale E. (eds) (1989). *Parameters of Military Ethics* (McLean, VA: Pergamon-Brasseys).

MccGwire, Michael (2000). 'Why did we bomb Belgrade?' *International Affairs*, Vol. 76, No. 1, January.

Mileham, Patrick and Willett, Lee (eds) (1999). *Ethical Dilemmas of Military Interventions* (London: Royal Institute of International Affairs).

Miller, Richard B. (1991). *Interpretations of Conflict: Ethics, Pacifism and the Just War Tradition* (Chicago and London: University of Chicago Press).

Montor, K. (1995). *Ethics for the Junior Officer* (Annapolis, MD: Naval Institute Press).

Paskins, Barrie and Dockrill, Michael (1979). *The Ethics of War* (London: Duckworth).

Prins, Gwyn (1998). *Strategy, Force Planning and Diplomatic Military Operations (DMOs)* (London: Royal Institute of International Affairs).

Roberts, Adam and Guelff, Richard (2000). *Documents on the Laws of War* (3rd edn) (Oxford: Oxford University Press).

Rose, Gen. Sir Michael (1998). *Fighting for Peace* (London: Harvill Press).

Wakin, Malham M. (ed.) (1986). *War, Morality and the Military Profession* (2nd edn) (Boulder, CO and London: Westview Press).

Walzer, Michael (1977). *Just and Unjust Wars* (London: Penguin Books).

Index

maturity, 69, 82, 97
obligation, 11, 67, 68, 69, 76
restraint, 5, 25, 28, 31, 61
scrutiny, 46, 83, 89
morale, 28, 43-7, 49-9, 61-9, 77, 97
Morillon, Gen. Philippe, 5
motivation, 57-9, 63, 76-7, 97
multinational operations, 22, 43-7
Muslim tradition, 8

national
capitals, 44, 47
cultures, 30, 31, 43, 44, 51, 76, 84
identity, 9
interests, 3, 25, 51, 53, 54, 72, 80,
83
legal tradition, 30, 43
sovereignty, 11, 33, 71
survival, 25, 27
NATO, 7-8, 11, 13, 18, 31, 33-41, 43,
72-6, 90, 96
Netherlands, 89
non-governmental organizations
(NGOs), 17, 45, 55
non-intervention, 33, 62, 81

Omdurman, battle, 2

Panama, 30
Paris Maritime Agreement, 23
peace support operations (PSOs), 4
'perfidy' 27
philosophy of life, 50, 52, 67
pilot
choice, 29, 31, 65
error, 29, 31
political consensus, 25-6, 51, 52
Pristina, 8
proportionality, 33, 35-8, 40, 44, 53,
80, 93

Rambouillet, 34, 72, 96
Red Cross (IRRC), 22-3

refugees, 11-12, 28, 43, 90
regimental tradition, 28, 58, 61, 68
'Revolution in Military Affairs'
(RMA), 34
'right and wrong', 28, 46, 55, 61, 63,
69, 97
risk-averse, 45
rules of engagement (RoE), 4, 27, 31,
34, 39, 43, 49, 55, 59, 62, 75,
82, 91, 94
Rwanda, 18, 21, 29, 75

SACEUR, 36, 40
Schwarzkopf, Gen. Norman, 30
security, 45
Serbs, 8, 31, 33, 35, 38-9, 73, 90
Sierra Leone, 13
Somalia, 21, 28, 31, 77
'strategic corporal', 28, 32, 62, 74,
79, 87, 91, 97
stress, 49, 63, 82

targeting, 30, 34-5, 37-40
territorial rights, 11, 51, 53
total war, 3, 25, 64

Ukraine, 9
United Kingdom, 18, 29
United Nations (UN), 10-15, 18-19,
43, 55, 75
Charter, 11, 13, 18
command structure, 12-13, 19
General Assembly, 19, 21
High Commissioner for Refugees,
14, 43
Secretary General, 19, 21, 75
Security Council, 10, 12, 13, 19,
21
United States of America
Air Force, 34-5, 37
policy, 22, 34, 36, 98
Marine Corps, 28
'unity of purpose', 44, 52, 53, 67

Index

Universal Declaration of Human
    Rights, 11
unmanned aircraft, 39

video-teleconferencing, 40, 41
Vietnam, 30, 36, 39, 95
'violence', 52, 54, 81

'warrior, the', 84, 87

weapons, precision, 34-5, 40, 73, 83,
    93-4
World War, Second, 37

Yugoslavia, 18, 19, 52, 89

'zero casualties', 31, 32, 83